Pocketbook
Power

Pocketbook Power

How to Reach the Hearts and Minds of Today's Most Coveted Consumers— Women

Bernice Kanner

AdvertisingAge

AdAge.com

McGraw-Hill

New York   Chicago   San Francisco   Lisbon   London
Madrid   Mexico City   Milan   New Delhi   San Juan
Seoul   Singapore   Sydney   Toronto

The **McGraw·Hill** Companies

1 2 3 4 5 6 7 8 9 0 DOC/DOC 0 9 8 7 6 5 4

ISBN 0-07-141860-1

McGraw-Hill books are available at special quantity discounts to use as premiums and sales promotions, or for use in corporate training programs. For more information, please write to the Director of Special Sales, McGraw-Hill Professional, Two Penn Plaza, New York, NY 10121-2298. Or contact your local bookstore.

This book is printed on recycled, acid-free paper containing a minimum of 50% recycled, de-inked fiber.

Library of Congress Cataloging-in-Publication Data

Kanner, Bernice.
    Pocketbook power : how to reach the hearts and minds of today's most coveted consumers—
women / by Bernice Kanner.—1st ed.
      p.   cm.
    ISBN 0-07-141860-1 (alk. paper)
    1. Women consumers. 2. Consumer behavior. 3. Marketing. I. Title.

HF5415.32.K36   2004
658.8'32'082—dc22

                           2003025366

The rising influence of women will be one of the most powerful transforming changes of this century.

MADELYN HOCHSTEIN, PRESIDENT DYG

I love being a woman . . .
I am a finisher
I am a mother
I am strong, feminine, and sexy
I define success
I celebrate life
I am a role model

MARY INDRITZ, ST. PAUL, MINNESOTA

Women are opportunity no. 1.

TOM PETERS IN *THE CIRCLE OF INNOVATION*

At the dawn of the twenty-first century, American women vocalized their power and began to exert it. In the last few years marketers have begun to recognize the power of the pocketbook—and to play to it. The women's movement in its broadest terms, which has transformed society, is at last transforming the marketing arena. Here's how some marketers have responded to her roar along with a road map to how to sell to women.

Contents

Part 1

Understanding the Incredible Purchasing Power of Women

1

What the Snake Knew: Women Are the Ones to Reach

The serpent in the Garden of Eden knew it first. Marketers caught on centuries later. Women are the ones to reach. Since Eve's time they've been the gatekeepers in the kingdom of consumer spending, the ultimate decision makers. Yet only recently have marketers really understood the extent to which women figuratively wear the pants. The implications of that realization have transformed the marketing world and, by extension, our cultural landscape.

A handful of professional media watchers still wring their hands over (and earn their livelihood from pointing out) "disturbing" images of anorexic, airbrushed, idealized beauties whom they claim drive normal women to compare and despair. Others whine about the relative invisibility of women on marketers' radar screens. Still others concede that women are represented all right—but complain that it is largely lip service or tokenism.

Leaf through a stack of magazines or surf the Web or TV, and sure as a robotic telemarketer interrupting dinner, you'll come upon pitches using women as pinups or promiscuous props. The Advertising Women of New York's (AWNY's) annual Good, Bad & Ugly awards found no shortage of contenders for the 2003 Grand Ugly. All too many marketers pressed "the stereotypical default button on men's fantasies, featuring bimbos and degradation," said Nancy Axthelm, executive vice president at Grey Worldwide and one of the AWNY judges.

Audacious, loutish ads crafted by the clueless, however, are either an endangered species or intentionally designed to titillate men. Men do, after all, still buy most of the beer and vacuum cleaners. What about all those perfect women in "aspirational" ads? Research suggests that most of us *like* to see them: We recognize the fantasy—and buy into it. And when we don't share the fantasy or we object to it, more often than not the advertiser gets the message and changes the pitch. Instead of 15-year-olds slathering on antiaging skin creams, these days, mature (albeit still beguiling) middle-agers are demonstrating the products. This is so because purchasers did not relate to the previous presenters.

Before I had children, I longed for a son, not because I had a special affinity for males but because I knew life would be easier for a he-child than for a she-child. My prenatal yearning is still common around the world—and in America. Historically, being a born a girl meant joining a sorority of second-class citizens. Now that I have a child of each gender, I know history is being rewritten to be "her story" as well, perhaps more so in this century. As an "advertising anthropologist," I see marketing reflecting these changes.

Indeed, the Y chromosome is embattled today. In his recent book, *Y: The Descent of Men,* Dr. Steve Jones, a professor of genetics at University College in London, contends that men have devolved to become the "second sex . . . a mere remnant of its once mighty structure." Writing in the *New York Times,* columnist Maureen Dowd contended that for years, men, feeling clumsy and insecure, have fretted "they may be rendered unnecessary if women get financial and biological independence, learning how to reproduce and refinance without them." One result is that men are becoming more feminized, thinking it is "better to be an X chromosome than an ex-chromosome."

On average, three sex change operations are performed every day in America. Almost all are male-to-female transformations. The figures that represent Liberty, Justice, and Wrath are female. There is no Mr. America. Granted, Cupid, Father Time, and Uncle Sam are guys, but many suspect that Santa Claus is a woman. How else could the red elf pull off that huge, organized, warm, fuzzy, nurturing social event called Christmas? And Dan Brown's *Da Vinci Code* jolted readers with its notion of feminist divinity.

After all, it wasn't that long ago that legendary adman David Ogilvy chided marketers for the ubiquitous practice of talking down to women. "The consumer is *not* a moron; she's your *wife*," he berated those who patronized or discounted them, those who misconstrued men's higher paychecks to mean greater spending clout. Yet even Ogilvy could not predict how pocketbook power dominates the world of commerce. It decides not only what and who to buy (politically and entertainment-wise) but also when and where to buy it (online, boutiques, department stores, catalogs). Women are even dictating to retailers what they'll pay.

The pocketbook holding this power must be pretty capacious: Women, who comprise just over 51 percent of the U.S. population, control $6 trillion in buying power annually, according to the Bureau of Economic Analysis. This is 600 times the amount of gold stowed in Fort Knox. Statistics compiled by the Women's Entertainment Network, the sales promotion agency Frankel & Co., and others suggest that all told women make 88 percent of the retail purchases in America. They buy:

- 53 percent of all stocks
- 51 percent of all sports equipment
- 66 percent of all personal computers (PCs) and 51 percent of consumer electronics
- 47 percent of hardware and home improvement materials
- 85 percent of toilet tissue
- 81 percent of groceries
- 75 percent of over-the-counter drugs
- 90 percent of greeting cards
- 94 percent of all home furnishings

- 46 percent of men's wear
- 60 percent of flowers
- 65 percent of all cars
- 80 percent of all health care
- 88 percent of medical insurance
- 60 percent of self-help books

Four of every five homes in America have been selected by a woman (Mediamark Research, Inc.), as have 7 of every 10 appliances (Grey Advertising). Women handle 75 percent of family finances (Publicis), initiate 65 percent of divorces (although *their* standard of living usually declines after the split, whereas their husband's rises), and write 80 percent of all checks. Demographers expect that by 2020, through inheritance, marriage, salary, or crook, women will control most of the money in America.

Already, 43 percent of people with assets over $500,000 are women. Men still earn more overall, but the gap keeps narrowing— from 68 cents to every dollar in 1985 to 75 cents in 2003 according to the Bureau of Labor Statistics (BLS). In addition, the BLS notes, one in every four wives earns more than her husband.

Worker Bees

Three of five women work outside the home. By 2005, women will comprise 62 percent of the nation's workforce, with increasing numbers on the upper rungs. In 2002, almost half of all managers were women—up from one-third in 1983. Catalyst's 2002 census shows that nearly 16 percent of *Fortune* 500 corporate officers are women, up from 12.5 percent in 2000. Almost 8 percent of them hold C level posts, up from 2 percent in 1995. Moreover, in 16 percent of large corporations, women head the in-house legal teams.

Besides scaling the corporate ladder, women are demonstrating momentum by swarming into heretofore male-dominated professions such as engineering and accounting and inching into enclaves such as architecture, computer analysis, construction, aviation, and even pest control. Roughly 2 of every 100 electricians and 1 of every 100 aircraft mechanics are female.

At the same time, women are also leaving corporate America at twice the rate of men, flummoxed by obstacles blocking their climbs in big companies, and becoming entrepreneurs, says Myra Hart, professor at Harvard Business School. Every 60 seconds nowadays a woman opens a new business. Collectively, women start businesses at 1.5 times the rate of men, according to the U.S. Department of Labor. One of every 11 American women now owns a business. Gender-wise, women own more than one-fourth of all the privately held firms in America, and by 2005, they will own more than 40 percent. The number of companies owned at least half by women is growing nearly twice as fast as all companies, says the nonprofit Center for Women's Business Research.

Many more small-company owners are considering their daughters as their successors, according to a study by Babson College, because of their degrees (half of all business bachelor's degrees and 40 percent of master's degrees now go to women) and qualifications, and with female CEOs in the spotlight, it's certainly not a choice from left field. Women also are often better at team building and communications, research shows, skills that are now valued more in business.

Indeed, two-thirds of adults think that their moms would do at least as good a job as their current CEO in dealing with employees, 62 percent expect that they would handle the corporate finances at least as well as their actual boss, and four of five think that they would do the job more ethically, according to staffing firm Ajilon Office.

McCann-Erickson has been, historically, a man's agency. I wanted the agency to add estrogen for people to "get in touch with their female side." I'm not suggesting men should weep in meetings, but they should embrace what we usually think of as female attributes: teamwork, relationship building, collaboration and empathy. That's the new paradigm for effective leadership, and mothers and wives have been doing this since time began. We're still competitive, but now we compete as to who is more collaborative.

Nina DiSesa, chairman, CEO, McCann-Erickson, New York

Not only do women collectively have the means, but they also have it longer than men. The average life expectancy of women is 79 years, compared with 72 for men. It is no surprise, then, that 80 percent of the residents at Sunrise Assisted Living are female. Men start out numerically superior and stay that way until their mid-20s. By age 30, the balance has tipped: There are 99 men for every 100 women. The gap widens with age. Three of every four octogenarians are female. Most are healthy, active, and handling their own business affairs.

Marketers of every ilk follow the money. The TV networks and newsweeklies have sniffed the scent coming from a different direction and are courting women, as are the makers of cars and truck, tires and motorcycles, scotch and screwdrivers, tech and telecoms, and even cigars, guns, and condoms. Women still rule the traditional female domains centered on home and hearth—food, furniture, and fashion. Now, however, they are suffering equal-opportunity heart attacks, enduring stress-related commuting, and watching Sunday sports. (Almost half the fans on Super Bowl Sunday are female, as are 40 percent of NASCAR buffs.)

Marketers weren't motivated by female activism: Women call or write their congresspersons or newspaper editors far less than men do. Rather, they've been drawn by the most obvious and compelling force: pocketbook power.

Instead of packaging "male" products in pretty pink boxes, marketers are creating wares with real points of difference or benefits. In 1996, not one product targeted specifically to women was launched. By 2001, there were 40, according to Mintel International Group, a new-product tracking company. The number was even higher in 2002.

When PepsiCo concocted fruit-flavored Aquafina Essentials, it spiked the bottled water with woman-friendly minerals and vitamins. The flavoring and packaging of Crest's Rejuvenating Effects toothpaste were designed for women by women (its three marketing managers were known inside Procter & Gamble as the "Chicks in Charge"). The ergonomic oval head and curved handle of Gillette's Venus razors were calculated to easily fit in a woman's hand. Hooker Furniture Company makes desks with higher work platforms to accommodate women who often cross their legs when working, a locking compartment for a purse, and a small velvet box so that earrings aren't misplaced when a woman answers the phone. And Sherwin-Williams' "Twist and Pour" Dutch Boy paint can was intended to be easy enough for finely manicured hands to open.

Women Stats (And We Don't Mean 36-24-36)

- Women are the better-educated gender.
- In a recent year, according to the National Center for Education Statistics, women earned 55 percent of bachelor's and master's degrees, 59 percent of associate degrees, and 40 percent of doctoral degrees. They also earned 53 percent of undergraduate degrees in biology and 46 percent in math and statistics. Women have earned more than one-fourth of the doctoral degrees in science for 30 years. Thirty percent of all lawyers and 42 percent of associates at large law firms are women, as are nearly half of students entering law school.
- The U.S. Department of Education expects college enrollment to be 57 percent female in 2007.
- Sigmund Freud got famous asking what women want; there's a good chance women will be the ones answering. Some 48 percent of psychologists are female, according to the American Psychological Association, and 75 percent of those earning bachelor's degrees in psychology are women, as are 66 percent of those advanced degrees in the field.
- Today more than 45 percent of new students at U.S. medical schools are women, as are 38 percent of all

medical residents, according to the Association of American Medical Colleges. And many more medical schools are enrolling more women than men in incoming classes.

Linguist Deborah Tannen took the publishing world by storm a few years back by articulating the differences in the ways the genders communicate. What is surprising is that everyone already knew it. Study after study shows that men and women perceive things differently, prioritize differently, and respond to messages differently. Want to motivate men? Try making competitive performance claims such as bigger, better, and best. Men like maximum amps, the newest models, and the highest return. Women, on the other hand, like to connect. Show them how something makes them a member of the sorority, solves a real or perceived problem, or magnifies the meaning in their lives. "You can't 'sell' to women so much as 'connect' with them," notes Carrie McCament, senior vice president and founder of Frank about Women. Indeed, Tannen claims that "women speak and hear a language of connection and intimacy, while men speak and hear a language of status and independence."

According to the International Mass Retail Association, brand characteristics and personal assistance from store personnel carry more weight with women than with men. Women value the "Made in the United States" label more than men do, and they pay more attention to coupons and promotions. RoperASW found that two of three women but only 15 percent of men are likely to switch brands because the company sponsors a cause they support.

Marketers recognize these gender differences, of course, but some worry about a price for honoring them. Years ago, advertisers refrained from casting blacks in commercials, fearful they would alienate white consumers. A similar trepidation prevents many manufacturers from "painting their brand pink." (Various research studies suggest that women also spurn pink for being condescending or overpriced.) Manufacturers fret that overtly pursuing women will squelch men's appetite for their brands. In fact, almost the opposite actually happens. When companies tinker with their products to meet women's higher expectations and do it without pandering, they please their male customers as well.

The trick, of course, is to deliver a message that cuts through clutter, convinces with charm and grace, and connects solidly with a fast-moving target. Women are evolving from a time when they were less willing "to subsume themselves or limit their ambitions to make life more congenial for men," says Andrew Hacker, a professor of political science at Queens College in New York. Even juggling is an antiquated term, suggests Anne Marshall, cofounder of WomanTrend, a Washington, D.C.–based market research and consulting firm. "My mother juggled. I'm choosing."

Women may choose to be full-time moms or serial careerists, to have children or jobs early, late, or not at all. They may choose to opt in or opt out. The new normalcy is that they are the ones choosing. Of course, their choices are greatly influenced by the economy, the political scene, and what's happening in the larger world and in their smaller, immediate one. Overall, the zeitgeist has created what J. Walker Smith, president of Yankelovich Partners research firm, calls "an undercurrent of anxiety . . . and an intense craving for comfort and connection." Women now are more interested in spending time with family and friends than spending money in malls and outlets. Increasingly, they recognize "housework" as something you do that no one notices unless you don't do it—and cooking from scratch as a Stone Age art from the days when big breasts were more important than thin thighs. Opinion Research Corporation found that almost half have demoted cleaning not because they have less time but because they feel there's more to life than cleaning.

Women are also more resistant to aggressive hucksterism. Advertising has to be "cute like an invited guest with something of value to offer," says Roy Spence, Jr., president of the GSD&M Agency in Austin, Texas. The offer must go beyond the obvious. Southwest Airlines is more than a seat to a destination, he says. It's about freedom. Wal-Mart is about democratization. It lets anyone buy the same things as rich people. "Krispy Kreme is in the 'magic moment' business, and the U.S. Air Force is in the winning business," he says.

Finding the right words to accomplish all this is no easy task. Marketers are learning to watch their language. General Motors, for example, meant well but executed a Catera commercial poorly, offending the very target GM was trying to woo. In the medieval fairy tale presented in its 1997 Super Bowl commercial for "the Caddy that zigs," Cindy Crawford played a beautiful but bored princess who wanted some magic in her life. The wizard she consulted advises her to get a Catera. Women (including GM's own female executives) were offended by the term *princess,* the unsubtle sexual innuendo, and Crawford's dominatrix outfit of black leather micro skirt and thigh-high leather go-go boots.

Marketers *know* that in today's world the fairytale prince may never materialize. Thus the "princess" will have to make her own way. More and more marketers are selling cars on safety, comfort, and style rather than on torque or wheelbase; software on solving problems and making connections rather than on state-of-the-art technology; and hotels on ambiance and experience rather than address and prestige. Somehow, Charles Revson's practice of ignoring calls from the bank president or ad agency while hustling to take one from a woman whose lipstick had smeared doesn't seem so loony. He used to rationalize this seeming oddity, explaining that women are the real bosses.

Pundits say that understanding the "fairer sex" is an older pursuit than questioning the meaning of life. There is a joke in marketing circles about the guy who asks his genie to build him a bridge. The genie tells him it's too difficult a task. Okay, says the guy. "I market to women. Tell me what they want." The genie snaps back, "Do you want two lanes or four?"

Clearly, women are reshaping the world in which we live. As their roles and attitudes evolve, they are creating extraordinary opportunities for smart marketers who recognize this and struggle to come up with new ways to reach them. Who are these new women, what do they want, and what is the language to court them—to touch their minds and hearts and ultimately their wallets?

2

Women Have Changed the Landscape

Men don't much like it, but they can't deny it: Our culture has been "Oprahfied." "Hard" news is squeezed into ever smaller spaces on a page or program dominated by human interest or entertainment stories. On the nightly news, Peter Jennings may report the latest findings on Botox along with the latest dispatch from Basra. The newsweeklies' coverage of breast cancer, bikini cuts, and bilingual education deliver the same message—that women are the audience. They're the swing vote in elections, the force behind the lineup change of the Olympics, and the reason why Sears went soft.

Morning is the only part of the day in which network TV audience size and profits are growing. Here, female viewers outnumber males by as much as three to one. CBS's *Early Show* booted cohost Bryant Gumbel because women found him cold and standoffish.

On the sports scene, the jock and TV anchor delivering the sports story are as likely to wear bras as athletic cups. The "boy binge" of Sunday afternoon sports is now coed. And while the Super Bowl has been hijacked by the distaff sex—43 percent of its viewers are female—women have their own Super Bowl of sorts: The Academy Awards is known as the "Super Bowl for Women." Like the big game, this media event charges top ad rates, but two out of three of people watching are women. This is not lost on advertisers, who you'd think would be after men. In 2003, American Express advertised at the star-studded awards for the sixth straight year, after bailing from the Super Bowl in 1999. In addition, Home Depot, home of Joe Tool-belt, advertised on the Academy Awards for the first time but has never run an ad on the Super Bowl.

Sports is a welcome diversion for women because the texture of their lives has become knottier since September 11, 2001. The terrorist attacks just have morphed "SUV moms" (formerly "soccer moms") into "security moms." Women who wouldn't think of owning a gun now approve the pilot in a commercial airline cockpit packing one. And the number of women enrolled in the National Rifle Association's courses has multiplied. Polls consistently show that women feel painfully vulnerable—and willing to forfeit some of their civil liberties to feel safer. Their support for defense and governmental strength is buoying the Republican Party, President Bush's chief political advisor, Karl Rove, has crowed.

Politicians have long sought the female vote. In 2002, when Thomas Birmingham campaigned in Massachusetts, he promised a largely female crowd that he would be "the greatest feminist governor" in the state's history and pointed to his accomplishments in day care, education, and health care as evidence. Candidate Steve Grossman cited his record of appointing women to key posts and his support for math and science training to prepare them in industries where women are underrepresented. Shannon O'Brien pointed to the investment training program she initiated to help women manage money.

Many women are focused on managing their own political campaigns. More women (six) serve as governors now than at any time before (one of the four elected in 2002 is Michigan's Jennifer Granholm, with three children under age 12). Janet Napolitano is Arizona's third female chief executive in little more than a decade. Conservative North Carolina elected centrist Elizabeth Dole to replace angry Jesse Helms as senator. California's Nancy Pelosi leads the House Democrats, the first time a woman in either party has held the top post. The 108th Congress included 63 women representatives and 14 female senators. Madeleine K. Albright, the first woman Secretary of State in 1997, has been succeeded in the inner sanctum by Condoleezza Rice. Hillary Rodham Clinton's book sold more than 1 million copies in its early days, fanning speculation that she would run for president in 2008. Most people expect that a woman will occupy the Oval Office by 2012.

Women who entered the political pipeline serving on city councils, school boards, and state legislatures are moving into congressional and governors' offices, notes Ellen Malcolm of EMILY's List, which helps finance female Democratic candidates. Regardless of party, women in office are likelier to concern themselves with health, childcare, and education issues more than crime and the economy, research from Rutgers University's Center for American Women and Politics shows. And they are likely to stumble on the same pothole: mistakenly telling voters what great moms they are when voters fear that they will put their family first and their constituents second, says Republican media consultant Bob Farrell.

Outside the political arena women are changing the way the world works. By pushing for alternative work arrangements (job sharing, in-office day care, telecommunicating, and flextime instead of 9 to 5 rigidity), they are humanizing the workplace more than feminizing it. Roger Herman and Joyce Gioia, coauthors of *Lean & Meaningful: A New Culture for Corporate America,* expect more office coffee bars and plant-festooned common areas with comfy sofas and mellow music as companies try to become more homelike.

This is hardly to say that women are all about bouquets and curlicues. They are also changing the hard-line military landscape. In a 2003 "we've been waiting for you" commercial for the U.S. Air Force, the family member who routinely repairs the malfunctioning satellite dish finds those skills a good fit for the Air Force's Space Command. The twist: The "repairman" is a she.

The Army, Navy, Air Force, Coast Guard, and Marines are still looking for a few good men. However, since the military went all volunteer in 1973, it has started looking for some good women too. One in every five new recruits is female. Already, 15 percent of active-duty military personnel are women—versus 11 percent during the first Gulf War. Women make up 19 percent of the Air Force, according to the Women in Military Service for America Memorial Foundation in Arlington, Virginia, and 15.3 percent of the Army, 14.4 percent of the Navy, 10.3 percent of the Coast Guard, and 5.7 percent of the Marine Corps. High-tech, sophisticated equipment has changed the nature of warfare: Women now fly fighter aircraft and serve aboard combat ships.

Even before America was officially America, women fought for it. Without official recognition, they carried water, acted as saboteurs, and nursed on Revolutionary War battlefields. They were wounded and killed in the Civil War and World War I, were demobilized after that war ended, and recruited again for World War II. Almost 10,000 served in Vietnam and more than 40,000 in the first Gulf War. One in seven soldiers deployed in Iraq is female.

An all-volunteer military means that marketing must do what conscription had done before. It means that instead of a stick, the forces must entice with carrots. In an ad in *Downbeat* magazine, the Army enticed recruits with the opportunity to continue to study music, travel, and jam with other first-rate musicians. The Navy makes its sea life sound adventurous and glamorous: "It's not just a job; it's a flight exercise in Hawaii, the Caribbean and Hong Kong."

Ads that overtly court women veer from the macho image the services have long cultivated. Natalie Ortiz, a 22-year-old Army specialist, loves pathology, medicine, and science. She is profiled in an "Army of One" ad. Instead of the steely Marine of old, a recent Marine Corps ad showed a curly-haired woman musing about her future.

Uncle Sam also waged a persuasion war to convince "reticent mothers" who have "aspirations, hopes, dreams and ambitions for their children" to endorse their enlistment, says Air Force Major Joe Allegretti, who works for the Defense Department's Joint Advertising Market Research and Studies Program. Ads featuring veterans describing how military experience helped anchor their civilian lives (teaching them stamina and follow-through, for example) aim to get the gatekeeper to sanction her kid's enrollment.

Women today are more interested in finances, more willing to talk about and explore their sexuality, and more comfortable pursuing indulgence, says Madelyn Hochstein, president of DYG, Inc. From cigars to bubble bath, if it's fun, it's worth pursuing. Women have made the kitchen more a place to indulge a hobby than to pursue a daily grind and the supermarket not just a food distributor but also a caterer.

Women are also changing the way America shops. Just as network TV has lost ground with women over the past decade, so has loyalty to brands—especially with parity products and those used furthest from their faces. One recent study found that 28 percent of women say that they are not at all picky about brands and that they switch frequently. This lack of steadfastness is expected to grow.

Women today are also "convenience addicts." Their desire to get it done and move on has given rise to 24-hour shopping, catalogs, fast food, and double-duty products. It has meant the finale for "three squares a day," replaced by a movable feast of dashboard dining.

Another change is the way marketers aim for men. Many categories where men are the principal buyers use "female cues," says Alan Treadgold, director of research at the Leo Burnett ad agency. "Home entertainment systems are increasingly being sold on the basis of so-called female attributes—the environment of the store, level of service and other intangibles instead of gadgetry and technical features. Car marketers are emphasizing the people driving—and what they're experiencing—rather than the car's specifications."

For years, all deodorant ads said was that this one works for 12 hours, this one for 18, and this one for 36, said Diggi Tompson, North American brand director for Unilever's Axe. "That was the wrong conversation." In zany introductory ads, a young woman sprayed Axe on a mannequin, which ended up arousing her comically. Her boyfriend charges onto the set and knocks the mannequin's head off ("Roger! We were just talking!").

Women also have changed what they are shopping for in men. "They want a lot more from men than ever before," says DYG's Madelyn Hochstein. Among the performance standards by which women are judging prospective mating material are appearance, sexuality, and provider of fun, romance, and sex. Provider of security and money has dropped way down, although achievement and success are important status symbols, says Hochstein.

Many women have stopped shopping. The number of American women living alone has doubled during the past 20 years, to 43 million, and they are no longer putting their lives "on hold' until they have settled down with a husband. "In the United States, more than half of single women own their own homes. That means they're the ones checking out power tools, purchasing homeowners insurance, choosing the brand of snow tires," says Ira Matathia, managing director of Euro RSCG.

They are also the ones to credit for making the hospitality industry hospitable. Women have always made the vacation plans; now they represent close to half of all business travelers, according to Westin Hotels & Resorts. They have literally brought hotels out of the dark ages, transforming their atmosphere, amenities, menus, and service style.

Another societal reverberation is the new androgyny, a move from gender gap to gender overlap with unisex clothes, haircuts, parenting, entertainment, and gender-neutral dating etiquette. The days when a guy couldn't tell a washer from a dryer are history. Husbands put in more than twice the hours on household chores than they did a generation ago, says John Robinson, a time-use expert at the University of Maryland. Men are also more involved with their kids; Koala says that its diaper-changing tables are as likely to be found in men's public bathrooms as in women's. And Mediamark Research says that men buy almost one in four frozen breakfasts, canned stews, nondiet colas, wart removers, and shampoo.

Keeping up appearances—and suffering for beauty—has gone gender-neutral. While women have embraced "mannish" pleasures, men have become more feminized, interested in celebrities and health, family issues, education, eating disorders, and cosmetic surgery—topics that once made up the "women's pages." (The number of cosmetic surgeries performed on men in the United States has tripled since 1997, according to the American Society for Aesthetic Plastic Surgery.)

Many stoic, self-denying, modest straight men know the difference between volumizing conditioners and botanical ingredients. They are not gay or bisexual so much as "metrosexual" and are led by British soccer star David Beckham, who sports sarongs and nail polish. (Even Harrison Ford wears an earring.)

Men buy skin-care items (sales have risen 10 percent each year in the past 5 years) and makeup (Menaji's mascara is called "lash gel"; its blush is called "contour"). Tampa Bay Buccaneer defensive halfback Ronde Barber figures that he spends more than $400 a month on honey-almond body polishes, minty pedicures, facials, and body scrubs. Guys whose dads drew the line at Aqua Velva are getting microdermabrasion, pedicures, eyebrow shaping, Botox injections, and body-hair waxing. They are visiting hairdressers (not barbers) and wine bars (not pubs). They spurn harsh soap but spend mirror time smoothing, painting, conditioning, glossing, masking, and scenting themselves with the new "just for men" cleansers, moisturizers, hair-styling serums and gels, sunscreens, and depilatories that have emerged. They shop at boutiques, exercise at the gym instead of play a sport, and wonder which pair of Bruno Magli shoes to wear. They understand thread count, manners, and pedicures and have leafed through Condé Nast's new shopping magazine for men.

One in four spa visitors is now male, so spas are trying to exfoliate their image as female retreats. They are providing big-screen TVs (tuned to sports), huskier scents (rosemary and mint in lieu of lemon grass, orange, and sage, which men find too sweet), manlier nomenclature (the Turnberry Isle Resort spa in Florida calls its regime "golf conditioning," and the Rancho Bernardo Inn's spa offers the "sports massage"), and heartier food (forget asparagus spears; Red Mountain Spa in Ivins, Utah, serves carnivorous buffets and "Call of the Wild" dinner entrées of rattlesnake and caribou).

Despite the feminization, marketers go all out to make sure that men know that their products are manly. The grooming aids come in sleek black packages or other rugged looks instead of pastels and florals. Ads for Suave for Men personal care equipment overtly set them apart from women's products. Two couples are chatting at a table when one man invites the other to join him going to the rest-room. En route, they chatter about the new haircut one of them got as their women look on, dumbfounded. "You're not a woman," inter-rupts a voiceover.

Interestingly, many of these male skin care products such as Nivea for Men advertise in "women's" magazines. Ads for *Glamour* claim that its readers spend more on men's health and beauty aids than the mostly male readers of *GQ* and *Details* combined.

The Al Bundys out there still beat their chests, brag about foot-ball, and engage in dodgy virility rituals. They have been driven to male-bonding enclaves, to zapping (with so little to watch now), and to the bawdy bad-boy "guyness" of "laddie culture." Saturated with Neanderthal doo-doo jokes and scantily clad bouncy babes, laddie culture is evident in such magazines as *Maxim* and such TV pro-grams as Comedy Central's *The Man Show*.

Marian Salzman, strategy director at the Euro RSCG ad agency, calls the "I am man; hear me roar, belch, guzzle" movement an in-your-face pushback against "the antiseptic dimensions of politically correct living . . . soft guys eating quiche and loving it." Yet she warns that it is not a backlash against women. Rather, it is a façade for men behind which to hide their confusion about what it is to be a man today.

Men's confusion is understandable considering how the seismic changes they've triggered have undermined the very soil on which men, indeed, everyone, stands.

3

What Do Women Want?
C.H.A.R.G.E.

Instead of "I am special," the mantra of women today is "I am me." Instead of going public, women are focused on privacy. According to Yankelovich & Partners, women are seeking fulfillment on their own terms.

As a rule, women are no longer shooting for superwoman status nor whining, "Woe is me." Instead, they are playing the hand dealt them and looking for ways to make things happen. DYG identified four aspirations of today's women. They want control, appreciation or respect, love, and meaning. However, there are two other critical components: happiness, as in "girls just wanna have fun," and good enough, that is, editing out, settling in, and accepting who they are and that good enough is often better than perfection. In other words, women want CHARGE:

Control
Harmony and love/relationships
Amusement/fun
Respect
Greatness/meaning/spirituality
Enough

What the Wife of Bath Knew: Control

A few years ago, researchers at the McCann-Erickson ad agency were stumped. Combat, an insecticide that came in neat plastic trays and killed roaches quickly with no mess, seemed just what the doctor ordered.

Yet Combat sat on store shelves while Raid sold and sold. The great mystery was solved when McCann-Erickson asked heavy users—downtrodden women in the humid South—to draw a roach and tell a story about it. Virtually all depicted the bug as a man who comes round when he wants something and leaves once he's gotten it. The women never said so directly, but Raid let them watch the roach—that is, their man—squirm and suffer. Raid gave them a feeling of control and an outlet for their hostility that Combat could not.

Study after study of happy people reveals that they share one characteristic, a sense of control of their lives, says David Myers, Ph.D., professor of psychology at Hope College in Holland, Michigan. The Wife of Bath knew this, and for many women, "The Wife of Bath" was the most significant of Chaucer's tales. While women-as-victim may have worked once when women really were diminished, the model today is women in charge.

Indeed, the research firm DYG found that an equal number of women think that they have the greatest influence on their own lives as who think that God and fate combined do. Women want to be thought of as competent, capable, and in control of their lives, says Madeline Hochstein.

Traditionally, women have been "in charge" at home. And they overwhelmingly still run their households:

- 76 percent do most of the laundry.
- 73 percent do most of the cooking.
- 70 percent do most of the housecleaning.
- 67 percent do most of the grocery shopping.
- 56 percent pay most of the bills.

Now they are also taking charge of their destinies, choosing their clothes, careers, and lifestyles. They compromise more out of love and less out of duty.

Women are taking control of the money. According to DYG, 83 percent of women claim that they are assuming more financial responsibility than ever before. Seventy percent swear that they would never let their husbands handle their joint finances alone. More than half have their own money stashed, apart from what they share with their mates.

Sometimes, wresting control of a situation is costly. Twenty-eight percent of women have quit a job or left a stressful situation to regain their footing. Two in five have pushed for more scheduling flexibility at work. One in three has transferred positions, and another 12 percent have turned down promotions to regain control.

Rather than waiting by the phone for the guy to call, women are directing the course of relationships, comfortable as pursuers as well as pursued. And they are raising the standards on what they require from prospective mates. Eighty-eight percent admit that they have raised the bar on what constitutes partner material. Achievement and financial security are a given. So is royal treatment. Two of three women say that they would only pair up with someone who treats them like a queen. At the same time, women are much less concerned about a partner's looks than they used to be.

However, they are concerned about their own looks—and are having their lips plumped, their fat liposuctioned, and their smiles whitened, brightened, and rightened. They are also calling the shots on the health of their bodies. Seven of 10 women say that they will solicit their doctors' opinions and then evaluate the information they have gathered and write their own prescription, choosing among conventional Western surgery, herbal remedies, and even acupuncture.

Women are also organizing their personal lives and the stuff in it. Cleaning may have lost its zest, but organization and the control that it brings are third behind losing weight and having fun among women's main goals in life, says Cathy Rings, vice president of marketing at Rubbermaid. "Life is so complicated now that we increasingly try to simplify it for greater control." In a recent commercial, women whose mates spent an unauthorized night out with the boys drop their guys' gear out the window. The possessions of the one whose wife used Rubbermaid containers remained intact; the others were not so lucky.

Of course, women know that there is a lot they can't control—sickness, death, accidents, and even how their kids turn out—but where they can exert an influence, they are determined to do so. Maternal micromanagement may be as great a trend (and threat to kids today) as maternal neglect, with moms programming their children's lives to leave as little as possible to chance. Control starts in utero (with scheduled C-sections) and even before with in vitro and other gynecologic interventions to conquer infertility. Women are determined to control the sweet hereafter too. A third of women with young children admit that they have spied on their babysitters.

Harmony and Love/Relationships

Who, being loved, is poor?

OSCAR WILDE

To love another person is to see the face of God.

LES MISERABLES

The Eskimos have 52 words for snow because it is so special to them. There ought to be as many for love.

MARGARET ATWOOD

Since when were *practical* and *romantic* mutually exclusive? Women still believe that love makes the world go round, but today they are no longer the sleeping princesses. They are activist-crusaders.

Because women can support themselves, they don't need to marry for money or security. Now they marry for love.

Relationship Wish List

Love may be blind, but it's not deaf. Among the biggest wishes that women have is that their mates listen better. They also wish that their partners would help out more. However, just 16 percent wished that their partners would be better lovers.

And marry they do. Despite rumblings about marriage, 70 percent of women still consider it the best arrangement available. Just 4 percent value their independence so much that they spurn any serious commitment.

Romance isn't the only kind of love they crave, however. They yearn for familial love. For 88 percent of women, their children are their greatest joy, and the loving bond they share is their greatest source of happiness. (Sixty-one percent who don't have children admit that they often wish that they did.) It is more the love they feel *for* their children than *from* their children that they find fulfilling. Women say that this connection with their children teaches them how to connect with the rest of the world. Four of five credit motherhood with pushing their own needs out of first place. And 61 percent say that their willingness to sacrifice for their children has made them stronger, better people.

Women also know that when Bette Midler rasped, "You gotta have friends," she told the truth. The flimsy *Divine Secrets of the Ya Ya Sisterhood* became a hit because of its substantive premise about the importance of friendships. The average woman shares her life with six close friends. Only 2 percent have no best friend. Surprisingly, as women age, they amass more friends. Two in five who call themselves happily married confide secrets to friends that they do not even share with their husbands. Hallmark has plugged into this girlfriends phenomenon by creating a line of Celebration of Women cards.

Amusement and Fun

> *Ever notice how "What the hell?" is always the right decision?*
>
> MARILYN MONROE

It's not just girls who want to have fun: It's grown women too. Study after study shows that whatever they're doing, women are more focused on enjoying the journey than on just getting to their destination, says DYG's Madelyn Hochstein.

Marketers are trying to make those journeys amusing and sensory. Apple made its iMacs colorful, stylish, and easy to use. "Somber" fragrances have gone playful. Once serious broadcasters now offer lively banter. And translucent plastic jellies in fuchsia and turquoise have made a comeback from the 1980s for the simple reason that they are fun.

Ikea's giant new stores—one occupies 30 acres in the Washington, D.C., area—propel shoppers around a racetrack-style showroom where living rooms blend into kitchens, which make way for work areas and so on, showing all its 80,000 items. "A big part of Ikea's winning formula is the fun of the shopping experience itself," says Christopher Gunter, president of the Retail Group in Seattle. Women crawl into the display beds with no salesman huffing at them, a supervised play area replicates a Swedish farmhouse and forest for the kids, and you can walk in, get a couch, and walk out instantly gratified. By making furniture "a fashion object rather than an heirloom, Ikea gives us permission to buy something that will wear out and that's OK" because it wasn't expensive, Gunter said.

Indulgences such as spas, bubble baths, champagne, personal shoppers, and special-occasion chefs have thrived even when the economy did not, as have fun sports equipment such as inline skates and snowboards and accessories such as spangled flip-flops and other "girly things."

The trick women face is to fit the good times in. Fully half of all women complain of time poverty, that they simply don't have enough time to do it all, according to RoperASW. Tension has become such a staple in their precarious juggling acts that many remind themselves that a day without stress is like a day without a heartbeat.

Marketers whose products can bust stress and elicit laughs have their foot in the door of women all too ready to lighten their loads and moods. Martha Stewart may have blown it by being greedy, but she led the crusade that turned chores into entertainment by making them fun.

Respect

When financial guru Suze Orman was small, her dad, a blue-collar laborer, brought her along when he went to Saks to buy a suit. Because he was shabbily dressed, no salesperson would wait on them. Disgusted, Orman's father decided to shop elsewhere.

The humiliation that Orman felt then turned into a seething resentment that may have fueled her drive and ultimate success. Why? Because Orman, like virtually all women, yearns for respect.

When Aretha Franklin belted out "R-E-S-P-E-C-T" in 1967, she hit a chord to which American women have long responded. Numerous studies show that, for women, the way salespeople treat them is every bit as important as the quality of merchandise they are mulling and even its price.

Many marketers have gotten the message. Banking centers, photo drop-offs, and pharmacies in grocery stores tell women that their patronage is valued. So do mini-fast-food restaurants in discount stores and at gas stations and coat checks, carts and caddies to haul packages to the car, and rest areas for weary shoppers to recharge at malls. The relaxing, comfy atmospheres in Borders, Barnes & Noble, and Starbucks have made them community centers.

Still, while 87 percent of men feel that they are taken seriously when they bring their cars in for repairs, fewer than half of all women think so. They believe that while a man's idiosyncrasies enhance his looks, a woman's detract from hers. Women also find sales and customer service staffers dismissive, patronizing, and condescending.

They are especially wary of those selling electronics, whom they suspect stereotype them as easy marks and try to intimidate them into buying pricier models or consider them unworthy of their time if they aren't knowledgeable enough to appreciate the gadgetry. Car service centers (admittedly an oxymoron) with smoky waiting areas, dirty plastic chairs, and a pile of dated *Field & Stream* magazines do not exactly lay out a cordial welcome mat.

Greatness, Meaning, and Spirituality

If you think you're too small to be effective, you've never been in bed with a mosquito.

BETTY REESE

Women today want their lives to mean something, to satisfy an inner hunger, even if it costs. Eighty-six percent say that they are far less concerned with what others think of them than they once were. What concerns them now is editing their lives to make more room for the grace notes and inner satisfaction: Eighty-five percent of women yearn to make a positive difference in the world, and 72 percent say that no job is worth it if it doesn't gratify them personally.

There are two ways of spreading light: to be the candle or the mirror reflecting it.

EDITH WHARTON

This quest for meaning has fostered an increased sense of spirituality (versus religiosity). Eighty-three percent of women call themselves spiritual, drawn by the lure of inner peace, less stress, connection with others, and acceptance of death. Savvy advertisers such as Rider Jeans with its "I Am Beautiful" campaign play back to women the theme that outer beauty comes from within.

This quest has spurred self-growth programs and "culture-tainment." Women are taking courses, reading, and choosing educational vacations over restful ones. They are fueling the growth in educational TV, exotic foods and travel, and museum visits.

Good Enough

A dinner party is the litmus test. Some 81 percent of women hosts mingle with their guests and let the food be good enough. Only 18 percent slave in the kitchen to be sure that the food is spectacular.

With simplification being the goddess and her subjects editing their to-do lists, good enough regularly beats out spectacular. Almost every decision a woman makes is subject to split-second analysis: How much time, effort, and energy must I put into this? Does it add stress to my life or bring me more of the good stuff I need?

As they shift from working harder to working smarter, women seek out companies that are part of the solution, not part of the problem. More women are tossing out perfection to do just enough to get the payoff. More than half of those in the workplace say that they've got a job, not a career.

The only area where women are unwilling to sacrifice is motherhood. All others are open for negotiation. Take housekeeping. There aren't many floors you can eat off anymore, and this suits women just fine. Surveys show that warm and cozy surpasses neat and clean as important home descriptors by more than three-to-one odds. Almost half of women concede that their cleaning standards have eroded over time and that their home is dirtier than the one where they grew up. But that's because life beckons. A Kimberly-Clark survey found that 45 percent of women cut back because "there is more to life than cleaning."

Good enough is, well, good enough in other areas too. Women want to do less work to look good. Overwhelmingly, the top criterion in selecting a hairstyle is that it is easy to maintain. Only 44 percent of women interviewed by DYG said that looking great all the time is important, compared with 68 percent who felt this way a decade ago.

Women Losing Zest for Cleaning House

Women's zeal to keep their homes clean is fading faster than ring around the collar after a bout with Wisk. The image of Mom bending over the ironing board or mopping the kitchen floor now seems as outmoded as a Norman Rockwell Thanksgiving, a recent Black & Decker Corporation survey suggests. One in five women will do almost *anything* to avoid housecleaning. Most clean reluctantly and perfunctorily; few do it zealously—or religiously.

Terry Carlson, manager of cleaning products at Black & Decker's household products unit, says that women's relaxed attitude toward cleanliness reflects the changing role of the home from a castle that once symbolized upward mobility to a life center, a nucleus of experiences, and a symbol of personal values. In other words, it is safe for slobs to let their hair down.

Today, "wash 'n' wear" and dry-clean-only have rendered the iron almost obsolete, and lightweight Swiffers have put the kibosh on mop wringers and hand-scouring floors. And women who once cleaned from room to room or performed one task at a time through the entire house today most often clean on the fly, with no particular pattern. This means that they want (in addition to a more participatory partner) anything that saves them time and energy.

When you think about it, the elements of CHARGE (control, harmony and love, amusement/fun, respect, greatness/meaning, and enough) are pretty good guidelines and assessment tools for men as well as women.

4

Finance:
Show Them the Money

Among the startling discoveries of recent times: Sheep can be cloned, wine can clear arteries, and women can handle money. This last discovery, coupled with the realization that the checkbook balancer can be a dollar averager, has prompted what Bloomberg's Susan Antilla calls "a near revolution" on Wall Street as marketers scramble to woo the gender "that heretofore had been more closely linked to tending to the electric bill than to picking the sector fund most likely to succeed."

Visions of a future as a bag lady still haunt one in every four women, even rich ones. However, most women know that it is up to them to make sure that this nightmare never materializes. Squelching intimidation, they are forcing themselves to learn the language of finance and all its subtleties. According to *Money Magazine*, 85 percent of women think about money more than they do about sex.

Perhaps this is because they *have* more of it. Women control 60 percent of all the wealth in America, according to New Fund Matters. The Internal Revenue Service figures that women make up 43 percent of taxpayers with gross assets of at least $500,000. By 2010, three in five women will earn more than their partners, predicts the U.S. Department of Labor.

At some point in their (compared with men, longer) lives, 90 percent of women singly will have to deal with the money they have earned, inherited, or received through divorce, says American Express Financial Services. Today, widowhood starts on average at age 56.

There is no shortage of advisors (books, magazines, Web sites, seminars, and corporate helpers) eager to show women with the monetary will "the way" to use it. Suze Orman, who tells the story of losing her first $1000 in a poor investment, has sold more copies of her financial guides than John Gray's *Men Are from Mars, Women Are from Venus*. (And Martha Stewart's fiscal miscalculation earned her more notoriety than any cherry cobbler she'd ever concocted.)

In 1997, marketers at T. Rowe Price followed a hunch. They put women on the cover of their brochures and mailed them out. Response from women to the mutual fund's mailer was 40 to 50 percent higher than before. Soon after, women began showing up in T. Rowe Price's magazine ads.

American Express' learning curve was more intense. By 1982, when 40 percent of the eligible universe already carried its basic green card, Amex cast about for ways to expand that share. Focus groups with career women offered a startling insight: The participants enjoyed Amex's long-running "Do You Know Me?" campaign but never imagined that the credit card was for them. "They saw it as a male product," said Shelly Lazarus, then director of the advertising account at Ogilvy & Mather and now CEO of the agency.

In the "Do You Know Me?" ads, high achievers whose names often were better known than their faces would recount an exploit ("I was the first man to climb Mount Everest"), state a problem ("I still forget to change my dollars into dinars before going to Nepal"), and explain why they carried the card ("It's recognized around the world"). Achievement for women, the Amex ad team discovered, meant living an interesting life, one that cuts across traditional roles.

In 1982, Amex swallowed corporate misgivings and served up the card as "part of a lot of interesting lives." Its campaign seemed to eavesdrop on real-life situations where the product name is offhandedly dropped in snippets of conversation. In one print ad, a cross-country skier nestled her infant in a Snugli. In others, a working woman leaves a sporting goods store clutching her attaché case in one hand and a lacrosse stick in the other, a businesswoman strides from a plane coddling a teddy bear, and a woman playfully invites her mate to dinner to inaugurate her first card. "I hear you can use it to take your husband to Paris," he teases.

"Interesting lives" clicked with women: Swarms mailed in their $35 application fee. It was a sharp contrast to earlier stumbles, which included a chauvinist cigar smoker advocating women getting their own Amex cards so that they can take him to dinner, a sexless ladder-climber advising that "to get anywhere in business" she'd need "a little application," and an icy airborne superwoman freezing out her seatmate by burrowing into her briefcase.

"It was tricky to not condescend to women and not to threaten men," said Lazarus. En route to "interesting lives," Amex scrapped superwoman stereotypes (the skin diver who's also a brain surgeon, mother of four, and bread baker) to avoid demoralizing potential enlistees. And it jettisoned such provocations as "A woman's place is in the kitchen," in which body copy set things straight (what if readers bailed before the record got set straight?). And it never presented the card as hero: It was an unspecified part of a lot of interesting lives—but never promised to find Prince Charming or make the bearer beautiful.

More recently, Republic Financial Services beckoned women with an ad explaining that it created its "Investment Lounge" because busy women "don't have time to properly investigate all the investment alternatives available today." An exuberant black woman in a State Farm Insurance ad details some of "3000 reasons to visit your State Farm agent." A board game in an ad for MassMutual shows the journey from "daddy's girl" to own woman. "We all start off dependent. Who makes it to independently wealthy is anybody's guess," the copy reads. "Along the way we can help you choose the right financial strategies . . . to be ready for whatever life spins your way. You can't predict. You can prepare." MassMutual also aimed to empower with the tale of a girl who "Never kissed a frog. Never had to." After she "bumped into the glass ceiling," Ms. Ambition "started her own business."

One of the five women in a recent Phoenix Wealth Management ad is about to do an initial public offering; another outearns her chief executive officer husband. First Union (now Wachovia) tried to quell a common female fear of outliving their money. Ameritrade Inc. tried flattery to lure women to its low-fee Internet brokerage: "After trying several different brokers, I finally found a stock market whiz—me," declares a very average-looking woman. The Discover card tells women, "You are the CEO of your life."

Paine Webber offers "investor education," and Salomon Smith Barney offers "Healthy, Wealthy and Wise" seminars to women that teach rather than sell. Vanguard and Scudder Kemper Investments distributes booklets and how-tos. Forty percent of Salomon Smith Barney clients (and its CEO) are women, up from 28 percent in 1995, after the investment giant went wooing. Merrill Lynch sponsors the Women's Sports Foundation, the LPGA, and a women's Web site. Attendees leave Oppenheimer's "What Every Woman Should Know about Investing" seminar with a book disproving myths about female investors—and a letter from its female CEO. (The firm counts 1.2 million accounts from women, up from 270,000 in 1993, when it first started targeting women.) Citigroup's Women & Co. launched in 2000 with ads showing designer jeans and shoes with tags such as "IRA" and "mutual fund," suggesting that there are better places to put money than in your closet.

More ads are touchy-feely and funny instead of crammed with interest-rate quotes. Washington Mutual uses ads to set itself apart from impersonal banks that track their customers via head scans or charge them a fee to use one of their pens. And Citigroup's "Live Richly" commercials, like MasterCard's "Priceless" commercials, remind customers that there are more important things in life than money. "Diversify . . . your friends," one billboard reminded. The goal, says Anne Bologna, director of planning at the Fallon ad agency, was to "tap into people's feelings and emotions around their finances."

Facts on Women and Finance

- Thirteen percent of married women have bank accounts about which their husbands know nothing.
- The average woman got her first credit card at age 25.7—4 months after the average man did. At 20.6 years of age, the average woman opened her first checking account (versus 19.9 years for men). By 16 years of age, 31 percent of American women (and 43 percent of men) had savings accounts in their names. And the average woman bought her first stock, bond, or mutual fund at 29.9 years of age, 2 years and 8 months after the average man.
- Sixty-two percent of women usually balance the family checkbook, 58 percent pay the household bills, and 44 percent balance the budget on their own (versus 23 percent of men), according to Oppenheimer Funds.
- The Web has changed the way people shop for insurance, says Jonathan Knowles, senior vice president for consultancy at BrandEconomics. "They start with the cheapest until the hit the only one they've heard of."

Those most likely to be in marketers' crosshairs are nearing retirement. At 38 million strong already, with one turning 50 every 7 to 8 seconds, women nearing retirement are the most populous group—and the neediest. Two of five women found the process of preparing for retirement "too hard to negotiate," says Don Blandon, president of the American Savings Education Council. "Many did not know where to start, or were uncomfortable dealing with financial institutions, or believed Social Security or family would take care of them." And only a third of women who have saved for retirement believe that they have invested wisely, compared with about half of men, according to the Retirement Confidence Survey. Seeing opportunity, companies such as MONY Life Insurance Company, Aetna, Inc., UNUM Corporation, and New York Life

Insurance Company have set up products and programs just to soothe them.

The programs take into account the different investing styles of the genders. A Wall Street adage has it that men worry about getting a good return on their money, whereas women worry about getting their money returned. Men tend to be more "abrupt and impulsive" investors. Rather than riding the bunny hill several times before tackling the double diamonds, they plunge in, taking risks, acting independently, choosing volatile "boy stocks" (i.e., high-techs, energy, and manufacturing), and exuding confidence because they are bluffing (or kidding themselves), says Paine Webber Vice President Mike Saunders.

Women, on the other hand, often suffer from "paralysis by analysis." They thoroughly research their purchases, lean toward "girl stocks" (i.e., retailers and consumer products), cling to their investment strategy, and often require hand-holding, according to the Investment Company Institute, a Washington, D.C., trade group for mutual fund firms. (Their approach seems to work. All-women investment clubs consistently outperform all-male clubs, according to the National Association of Investment Clubs. Still, women are far likelier to call themselves novice investors, whereas men are four times more likely to consider themselves experts, notes Gerry Myers, president of the Dallas-based Myers Group, which specializes in marketing to women.) Women worry more than men about having debt, so they are less likely to borrow or to sell equity.

Traditionally, securities sellers tried to make women feel dependent and insecure about their investing ability, says Carrie Schwab-Pomerantz. Daughter of discount brokerage pioneer Charles Schwab, Schwab-Pomerantz has overseen the company's women's initiative. "People, especially women, want contact with their money at all times. That led to our 24/7 Web and phone access," she said.

Women welcome financial advice, so long as it comes from someone they trust who does not talk down to them. Performance is a given in portfolio-land, says Linda Washington, founder of Allison Street Advisors. Beyond this, women want service and someone truly interested in their investment goals and personality.

An Oppenheimer survey suggests that they are not getting this. Fifty-eight percent of women think that brokers and financial planners treat them like Beanie Babies, and 54 percent of men agree that women are treated with less respect. *Money Magazine* found that just 27 percent of women and 31 percent of men say that financial advisors treat the sexes equally. Elise Scroggs, president of the International Division of Pliant Corporation, a Chicago-based plastics firm, likens the confusing experience of dealing with a financial advisor to going into an auto repair shop where "the guy says you need a new CV joint."

Women respond to financial marketing messages faster than men do, says Paul Lucas, formerly marketing vice president at First Advantage Federal Credit Union. "Men need to see on average of 18 multimedia impressions to understand a product's benefits and make a decision; women need only 5 impressions." (Lucas changed First Advantage's marketing materials so that within 5 years its constituency went from 68 percent military-related and male-dominated to 8 percent military-related and overwhelmingly female-dominated.)

Lucas likens banking to dating. "Men do it for convenience; women because of value," he says. While women investors often require more attention, the payoff is greater loyalty if they like the service, says Lynn M. Schmidt, president of Meritus Financial Group, a financial planning firm. "Men want less information, but they are less inclined to stick with the plan. They switch around a lot. Women want more education and take longer to make a decision. But they'll stick with the plan and remain loyal to you."

To score with women, banks and credit unions should couch everything in terms of service and demonstrate how it relates to life events, such as sending the youngest kid to college, buying a first home, or starting a business rather than listing the product's features, advises Tom Moseman, senior vice president at behavioral marketing research company Envirosell. This means convenient hours and locations, no lines, tellers who know you by name, and some entertainment for kids, such as lollipops or coloring books in the waiting area within parents' sight in a contained area away from doorways.

The widespread reopening of full-service bank branches was female-instigated. Bank One Corporation, Bank of America, Wells Fargo, National City Corporation, and Washington Mutual, to name a few, are again making automobile and housing loans, opening checking accounts, and even counting change, mundane services they jettisoned a decade ago to focus on investment banking and venture capital. Mergers forced them to slash costs, but their bare-bones strategies alienated customers.

Now banks are doing away with the velvet ropes and bulletproof glass and making free checking and online bill paying all but standard. Sunday hours, blender giveaways, espresso machines, on-premise dry cleaning, and comfy seating are also much more common. Washington Mutual has gone deskless but has added a kids' play area and roaming tellers who take orders to become an "unbank," says Chief Marketing Officer Brad Davis.

Commerce Bank, now open 7 days a week, offers free toasters, change machines, red lollipops, and massages on site. Employees with umbrellas usher patrons to their cars in the rain. There's a café, live studio, trading floor, and 100 laptops and plasma TVs in E-Trade's sprawling Manhattan center. Chief Knowledge Officer Connie Dotson says that it's all about giving customers choice.

Don't boast about your bigness, however. Nationwide Financial Services had fallen into the trap of talking about its size, admits President Joseph J. Gasper. Yet the life insurance and retirement-savings company caught itself and switched to telling folks what it can do for them. "Research told us that customers aren't interested in bigness but ache for personalization."

Women aren't just making more money than ever before (as well as spending and investing it), they're also moving markets—including money markets.

5

Wheels:
In the Driver's Seat

Not so long ago, the car lot was an extension of the men's room. Women were seen more often there in garters and bustiers on service area pin-up calendars, draped across a car hood in promotions, or on the arm of a male customer than solo. Her opinion, when solicited, was probably about the car color or upholstery.

Today women negotiate the wheel drives and financing for 60 percent of the vehicles on the road—both cars and trucks—according to J. D. Power & Associates. And they influence four out of five new vehicle purchases.

Collectively, women prefer different makes than men. Tom and Ray Magliozzi, hosts of National Public Radio's *Car Talk*, consider the Ford Mustang the "ultimate guy car" and the VW Beetle in ice-cream-shop colors tops for "chicks." Women also own nearly 7 of every 10 Chevrolet Cavaliers on the road and 64 percent of Saturns. Women buy 60 to 70 percent of all small cars, and they're a lot more interested in hybrids than men are, according to J. D. Power. Men are intrigued by their technology but worry that they won't perform. True sports cars, what the industry calls "luxury models," and full-size pickups, on the other hand, have testosterone in their tanks.

American men are likelier to buy an import; women are likelier to buy American.

This is, of course, an oversimplification because automakers are discovering that while safety, security, and reliability still appeal to women, they are also increasingly drawn to power, speed, and the hot looks of a screaming purple dragster. The aftermarket "tuner industry" of turbochargers, spoilers, and xenon headlights celebrated in *The Fast and the Furious* is beginning to woo women just as it does men. "The chasm between the sexes is getting less defined," said Ernest J. Bastien, corporate manager for U.S. vehicles operations for Toyota.

Even in the early days of automobiles, women weren't entirely cold-shouldered, although the clumsy, patronizing marketing steps may have made it seem that way. In 1911, Ford suggested that its wheels were "as easy to drive as the old family horse" and would be a tonic to make women's "worries vanish" and provide "exercise and excitement . . . relief from the monotony of social and household duties."

As women won rights, they also won ad visibility. A 1924 spot showed a businesswoman whose "habit of measuring time in terms of dollars" gave her "keen insight into the true value of a Ford." During the 1940s rise of suburbia, ads proposed purchasing one Ford for the breadwinner and its mate for the bread maker. A dimwit in a 1947 ad admits that she doesn't "know synthetic enamel from a box of my children's paints, but if synthetic enamel is what it takes to make that beautiful, shiny Ford finish, I'm all for it!"

In 1954, Chrysler unveiled a dusty rose La Comtesse model beside its bronze and black masculine counterpart, Le Comte. Women shrugged. In 1955, Dodge offered the two-door La Femme with pink seats and steering wheel and a leather makeup purse with lipstick, comb, and vanity mirror as standard equipment. Women yawned.

Pontiac's pink Parisienne, Cadillac's "girlied up" Eldorado Seville Baroness, and the feminized Martinque Impala also drew tepid reactions, even as General Motors hired nine "damsels of design" not "to add lace doilies to seat backs or rhinestones to carpets but to make the automobile usable and attractive to both men and women," Suzanne Vanderbilt, one of the original "damsels," said in 1957. "Women associate cars with masculinity and power," said Virginia Scharff, author of *Taking the Wheel*. "Given a choice between La Femme and a Barracuda, they'll choose the Barracuda."

Even as late as 1996, Cadillac miscalculated its audience and quickly canned a spot it created expressly to attract women who buy half the Cateras—double the sales of any other Cadillac model. It showed Cindy Crawford as a bored leather-garbed dominatrix-princess in a tight minidress with plunging neckline and knee-high leather boots.

Scorched by 1970s feminism, automakers began putting women in the driver's seat instead of just the passenger's seat and focusing on features important to them, such as safety and reliability. More-over, in addition to the traditional glamour shot of a car racing along a serpentine road, they began to show interiors too.

The showroom, factory, engineering studios, and ad dens were turned upside down. Car companies recruited women to weigh in on everything from the width of steering wheels to the placement of airbags. When GM discovered that the height of the step on some of its sport utility vehicles made for awkward clambering, they lowered it. Male executives had to motor around wearing paper clips on their digits to simulate how it felt to drive with long fingernails.

Art Redmond, executive director of global consumer insights for Ford, says that lumbar supports, adjustable seatbelts and pedals, and sensors that detect obstacles while reversing—all almost stan-dard now—were instigated initially by feedback from women. Ford installed child-friendly dome lights on minivans and manicure-friendly door handles on SUVs. Hooks for grocery bags cropped up in cargo bins, and mirrors dropped down so that drivers could check on kids in the back. Rectangular cup holders accommodated juice boxes. Lexus installed a purse holder in one of its models, and the third seat of a Mercury Mountaineer (60 percent of whose owners are women) adjusts with the flick of a wrist. The BMW's "Active Seat" massages the driver like a moveable spa.

Because of Mazda's misses, the sliding doors on its Special Edi-tion Sports F minivan have assist grips, and its sun visors slide to shield shorter people. Saab's Female Reference Group angled for more legroom under the steering column and easier-to-handle car jacks. Female focus groups drove Land Rover to improve its rear seats, rear door, and child seats, according to its marketing research manager, Paul Montopoli. Volvo's My Concept Car was conceived by an all-women team, and Ford's "Windstar Moms," a group of 30 engineer-mothers, convened to modify the 1999 Windstar, giving it a larger fuel tank for less frequent gas stops, a thinner steering wheel, and "sleeping baby" floor lights.

Women approach root canals and shopping for a new swimsuit with the same disdain they have for shopping for a new car, says Donna Kane, head of Hyundai Motor America's Power of the Purse program. Their key peeve: When the salesperson directs his or her questions to the man or patronizes her. At conventions, Hyundai distributes pamphlets on how to bargain in the showroom and make the test drive most effective. Saturn upped its female sales staff to 16 percent (versus an industry-wide average of 7 percent) and devised its no-haggle policy because women hate to dicker. And Volvo developed the world's first "virtual" crash-test dummy of a very pregnant woman.

(Women hold around 7 percent of all jobs in dealerships, up from 3.5 percent in 1990, according to CNW Marketing Research. However, while they account for 60 percent of the office staff, they fill only 7.1 percent of the general manager roles and 4.9 percent of the ownership positions, numbers that haven't changed much in the last decade. CNW says that 39 percent of women would rather deal with women in the car showroom versus 10 percent of men who prefer to buy cars from other men. On the flip side, 13 percent of women prefer to deal with men, and 11 percent of men want to deal with women. The rest are indifferent about the salesperson's gender.)

To promote Regals, Buick teamed with Sears and the Women's National Basketball Association. Jaguar was the exclusive automobile sponsor of the National Association of Women Business Owners. Chrysler made a multimedia deal with Martha Stewart, sponsoring her radio and TV shows, magazine, and Web site.

Subaru began a full-court press in 2000. Initial ads showcased tennis ace Martina Navratilova, golf's Julie Inkster, and Olympic skier Diann Roffe-Steinrotter; follow-ups featured mountain biker Tara Llanes and pro snowboarder Victoria Jealouse. In 2002, Subaru ousted Paul Hogan after 6 years "to associate more with the independent-minded and spirited character of our customers," said Vice President for Marketing Mark Darling. In one ad, an urban couple let their pooch pick which car to take to the hills, his SUV or her Subaru Forester. You know what the dog chose.

Jeep raced after women with movie trailer-like ads starring videogame heroine Lara Croft (Angelina Jolie) from *Tomb Raider*. She eludes pursuers in her tricked-out Jeep Wrangler Rubicon. In another spot, a woman tosses mud onto two Liberty Jeeps to decide which color looks better splattered, as she plans to get it. Ford's Expedition hired feisty boxer Laila Ali, daughter of boxing legend Muhammad Ali, as its spokesperson.

Mercedes-Benz parked its SL convertible on a fashion runway with ball-gowned models and sold its C Class sedan as a "man trap." In one spot, a love-struck bus passenger tosses his name and phone number into the open sunroof of a woman's Mercedes. She crumples it into her glove compartment, jammed with other discarded notes from admirers. Ford paired with "fashionistas" Carolina Herrera and Diane Von Furstenberg to design outfits to go with its new Thunderbird convertible. The car-and-clothes tableaus were showcased in women's magazines and auctioned to benefit breast cancer research.

Even "macho" models are revving to roll into women's garages. Porsche abandoned locker-room-type jokes and testosterone-driven headlines to show a couple languorously driving to a country bed and breakfast. Almost a third of those buying its Boxster and 911 models are women, 10 times the number just a few years earlier.

In 2003, Alfa Romeo traded its historically sexy image to plug dependability, safety, style, and durability. "Beauty is not enough," claimed ads where everything in an imaginary world is gorgeous but flighty, except for the Alfa 147, which powers around floating objects. Its driver is a self-assured woman in stilettos. In the past when Alfa

Romeo used women in its ads, "it was more for the men to like them," admitted Alfa Romeo spokesman Hans Hoegstedt.

Despite a hefty sticker price ($49,190), a sour economy, their military overtones, and an SUV backlash, sales of Hummer 2 have hummed along, with women snapping up over 30 percent of the vehicles. Hummer 2 has safety written large. "Women like a lot of sheet metal around them and see the Hummer as a defense mechanism," said Ad Director Liz Vanzura. They also see them as an aggressive tactic. In one spot, a woman steers her Hummer 2 through city streets while the narrator urges her to "Threaten men in a whole new way." (There are also male-targeted ads.)

Hard to climb into and maneuver, pricey to gas up, and bumpy to ride in, SUVs began life gunning for guys. They wound up winning over gals. One of eight automobiles sold in the United States in a recent year was an SUV, and women bought nearly half of them (albeit primarily the compacts such as the Chevy Blazer, Ford Escape, and Jeep Liberty).

Women like the roominess, adventuresome personality (versus the "soccer mom" minivan), and elevated perch of SUVs. Even small folks feel big up there. And they relish the power and how they look in them.

Still, with the increasing heat beamed at the gas-guzzlers, some SUVs, such as Chrysler's Pacifica, have crossed over. "Think of it as a cocktail with different ingredients, like a sport utility, minivan, and sports car," said Michael F. Donoughe, a DaimlerChrysler vice president. Ads using Celine Dion calmly practicing music in the passenger seat as the Pacifica powers through a rainstorm have women in their crosshairs.

Have Wheels, Will Go

Home may be where the heart is, but a driver's car is her castle. Women spend more time in their cars than the average American spends talking, playing sports, or eating, according to the Surface Transportation Policy Project's Nationwide Personal

Transportation Survey and the Americans' Use of Time Project. Everyone is driving more, but women (whether they work outside the home or not) are driving *much* more, chauffeuring kids and running errands. Women drivers spend, on average, 64 minutes a day behind the wheel—more than twice as much time as the average mom spends with her children.

In addition to deemphasizing features such as a unibody steel frame to celebrate the experience of the car instead, marketers have changed the tone of their ads depending on whom they are pitching. An ad for the Chrysler Town & Country minivan showed a sleeping toddler hugging a miniature van—a new kind of "security blankie." In the same month, an ad for the sporty Chrysler 300M in a men's magazine pictured a winding empty road, a thwarted state trooper, and the driver's smug smile.

For men, the ultimate dream is a Corvette, Ferrari, or other sports model. For women, it's a pair of diamond earrings. "We want women to view a Jaguar as a beautiful piece of jewelry," said Sue Callaway, general manager for Jaguar North America. Jaguar isn't the only luxury brand trying to be a girl's best friend. Saying that the BMW Seven Series sedans had proved too "sterile and Teutonic for many women," Thomas G. Jefferson, a BMW product manager, says that the interior of the latest model was made over to "look more like an elegant European living room than a car interior."

Before a woman takes title, chances are that she has researched a car thoroughly—paying more attention to capacity, reliability, safety, comfort, and image than to horsepower and torque—and made the vendor prove himself trustworthy, says Sandra Kinsler, editor of *Woman Motorist* magazine.

Unlike men, who aim to create a win/lose situation in the showroom, women would rather have a win/win situation, Kinsler says. Interestingly, it is women who are more interested in a vehicle's navigation and entertainment systems than guys are.

Price is critical with both men and women, and both expect financing deals and cash-back incentives. (In February 2003, the average incentive across the industry was $2135 per vehicle, up 41.3 percent from a year earlier, according to Edmunds.com, an online automotive information provider.) CNW Marketing/Research Vice President Art Spinella says that consumers won't consider buying a new car without a $3700 rebate, up from $2500 two years ago. Yet studies show that women typically pay more for a car than men, on average $500 more on a $25,000 vehicle, says Chris Denove, a partner at J. D. Power. The Internet is leveling the playing field by providing easy-to-access pricing guides and Web sites that let buyers bypass the intimidating negotiation process.

Lost in Space

Contrary to expectation, it is male motorists who are likelier than women to stop and ask for directions when they are lost (79.5 versus 60.9 percent), according to digital map developer Navigation Technologies. But women get lost less often, it found.

A car salesman scores with men by displaying his credentials and command of the product, often using technical jargon. This approach backfires with women, who see it as bullying and intimidating. "I've found that women don't want to be told they're different but like it if your product has a place for their umbrella or purse or seats that are easy to fold down instead of having to take them out," said James O'Connor, Ford Group vice president for North America marketing.

More and more of this low-key catering is the order of the day. Even when the salesman is a man, chances are that he's a "new" man, retrained to weed out preconceived stereotypes. A recent survey from Dohring Company in Glendale, California, found that women are more satisfied buying cars now than men are. Some 39 percent rated their car-buying experience as excellent, compared with 28 percent of men.

Fill 'Er Up and Fix 'Er Up

In a "Count on Shell" spot, a woman nods off at the wheel, and an oncoming car forces her off the road into a lake. "Would you know what to do?" an ominous voice asks before explaining how to get out of a submerged vehicle. In another spot, a tire blows on a busy highway, and the car veers dangerously close to an 18-wheeler. Again, the authoritative voice advises what to do (don't slam on the brake).

Vaguely reminiscent of Shell Oil's square-jawed Answer Man, a TV fixture for 15 years, the new know-it-all is more contemporary. His predecessor didn't "reflect the diversity of Shell's customers, and his glib ability to answer any question wasn't truthful," said Sixtus Oechsle, the executive in charge of corporate identity for Shell (which in 2003 appointed its first female CEO, Lynn Elsenhans). Women didn't cotton to him any more than they do to lab-coated doctors who once dictated what was good for them.

Shell and its rivals have undergone intense soul searching to redefine themselves closer to what its customers want from an oil company—a helpmate to the world rather than the god who controlled it. Texaco went to warm and fuzzy ads after an image doctor wrote a prescription, and Exxon began urging people to save the majestic tiger, its symbol for nearly 100 years, from extinction. Unocal 76 focused on the "little things" customers want from a service station, such as plenty of paper towels and squeegees.

The whole auto-related industry has awoken to women power. Quick-lube establishments and service companies such as Midas advertise in *Parents* magazine. Penzoil/Quaker State discarded spokesman comedian Denis Leary for actor Tom Berenger because the latter scored higher with women.

Tires

It wasn't just Ford's recall and replacement of 13 million tires after it investigated more than 100 deaths in tire-related crashes of Explorers in May 2001 that killed Firestone. It was women who ran the tire maker off the road because it did not restore their confidence in it quickly. Women resisted putting Firestones on their cars. They did *not* forgive or forget.

Fifty-one percent of all tires sold in this country are bought by women, figures Bob Tate of Welti & Call Advertising in Salt Lake City. With them in mind, Goodyear developed its Aquatreds and played up their safety features. Years earlier, in 1972, Dunlop introduced run-flat Denovos and marketed the tire as reassurance for women driving alone after dark.

Most tire ads present technical features, tread patterns, plies, stopping distances, and test and race results in a straightforward way. Stringent regulations prevent manufacturers from boasting about superior quality—but not from *implying* it. Instead of macho road imagery, since 1983 Michelin has used a tot playing in a tire. It raised the stakes of what's being protected, reminded viewers in an emotional way that "a lot is riding on [their] tires," and justified charging a premium for Michelins. In one spot, as "Jackie" frolics on a tire, a man tells his friend that he just bought a set of Michelins. "You could have saved some money on another brand," his friend replies as the tire swings back and forth. "Tell me the truth . . . didn't you buy them just for the name?" The owner agrees. "Yeah . . . the name is Jackie." (In 2002, Michelin bid baby adieu and brought back its anthropomorphic pile of tires. Michelin's new ad agency decided to woo "the high sport market" and light-duty truck owners who valued performance more than safety.)

"Girlz" Under the Hood

According to a legend floating around the Car Care Council a few years ago, when a woman complained that the auto repair shop didn't fix her air conditioning, the technician explained that women's body temperatures are higher than men's, which is why her car seemed too warm inside.

Nowadays, with women making up 65 percent of customers at service centers, such a response is likely to cause a big chill. Sadly, it's not all that uncommon. Four of five women are disappointed with the service they receive at service centers, and 89 percent complain that they are treated differently because of their gender. Indeed, while women rank automotive repairmen above plumbers and home maintenance contractors, just 21 percent consider them entirely ethical. When women find an automotive technician they trust, they stick with him more loyally than male customers.

Some companies *are* making an effort. "We've definitely noticed a lot more women bringing their cars in today than 10 years ago and are remodeling to make our stores more appealing," said Steve Steffens, vice president of marketing for Merchant's Tire & Auto. Under Merchant's system, the customer stays in her car, where "she feels involved, more in control, and more certain the work was performed."

Jiffy Lube is testing new waiting rooms with such amenities as Internet access, CD listening stations, TVs, phones, and a toy box for kids. "We've learned that anything we do to attract female consumers is readily accepted by male customers," says Marc Graham, president of Jiffy Lube International. "Women want more information than men about the repairs you're doing. If you intimidate her, or make her feel stupid, you've lost her. And if it will take more than 15 minutes of downtime while they wait for that oil change, we need to make her time productive."

More women today are even becoming Ms. Fix-Its, as automobiles become more computerized and technical and the work to maintain them less heavy and dirty. Forty million Americans do some of these repairs themselves, according to the Automotive Parts and Accessories Association. A fourth of them are women. And more than 6 in 10 women who own cars bought a part for it in a recent year, and they are as likely to pop the hood and install it themselves as to get someone to do it for them.

Women are changing wipers and batteries, checking and refilling fluids, and buying air fresheners, car wash products, floor mats, pin striping kits, tire care products, waxes, polishes, and wheel cleaners, says Mike Willins, managing editor of *Aftermarket Business*. "They may not be going after the hard parts yet, but they're interested in dressing up their vehicles and doing some of the lighter DIY stuff."

Motorcycle Mamas

"I'm old. I'm overweight. And when I'm on the bike, my butt hurts. My hands go numb. And I wouldn't trade it for anything." So says Carla Thibeault, a fifty-plus Middleboro, Massachusetts, office manager, mother, and motorcycle mama.

Motorcycling is still a young man's game—the incarnation of testosterone in metal and plastic. However, there are lots of biker "chicks" and grandpas too, lured by the siren song of wheelies. Between 1990 and 1998, the median age of buyers rose from 32 to 38, according to the Motorcycle Industry Council, whereas women accounted for 8.2 percent of all buyers, up from 6.4 percent before. While only 2 percent of Harley-Davidson sales in 1990 were to women, they now account for 10 percent. And while women drove off in 11 percent of Kawasaki's 500-cc sport bikes in 1996, their share roared to 28 percent in 1998. Roughly half of the enrollees in motorcycle driving schools are women, and J. D. Power & Associates found that 22 percent of people buying their very first bike were women. Women are the fastest growing demographic buying cruisers. (Harley created a "Rider's Edge" training program to teach women how to handle a bike and outfit themselves.)

Women aren't just important to the motorcycle industry as buyers: They are critical as "approvers." "Men may not like to admit this," says Ed Youngblood, president of the American Motorcyclist Association, "but many won't buy this 'man's toy' without a spouse, partner, or 'mommy' giving her stamp of approval."

Today, when it comes to anything with wheels, it's very possible that the customer driving the deal is a woman.

6

Health Care:
Our Bodies, Ourselves

In a TV spot, a young woman muses if, with her genes, breast cancer is inevitable. The pitch is for Salt Lake City biotech company Myriad Genetics to incite women like her to take its test and find out. Whether you consider this promotion irresponsible—after all, supposedly only 1 in 20 breast cancers have a genetic link and the DNA screen and required genetic counseling cost thousands of uninsured dollars—one thing you won't soon consider is that it is unusual. Today, ordering Myriad's test is as easy as buying flowers from FTD.com. It's one symptom demonstrating that the whole health care world has been reinvented.

Today, "women *are* the health care industry," says Bernadine Healy, former secretary of the National Institutes of Health (NIH) and head of the American Red Cross. They live, on average, 7 years longer than men, make at least 75 percent of all health care decisions, and spend 2 of every 3 health care dollars, according to the NIH.

Smith Barney says that women account for:
- Two-thirds of the 44 million hospital procedures performed each year

- Sixty-one percent of the 70 million annual doctor visits
- Seventy-five percent of nursing home residents
- Fifty-nine percent of prescription drug purchases
- Eleven of the 14 most commonly performed surgeries

Traditionally, women have been the caregivers. Now they are being recognized as the caretakers. Responding to female clout within the past decade, the Food and Drug Administration (FDA), the NIH, and the Centers for Disease Control and Prevention (CDC) established offices for women's health. Between 1996 and 2002, 19 states passed laws requiring health insurance companies to cover contraceptives. Gynecologic coverage, recently offered by less than half of fee-for-service insurers, has become almost universal. Drive-by mastectomies have been banned, and politicians use their support of health bills for women as a soapbox. In a recent year, 16 percent of NIH funds went to study diseases exclusive to women, three times the amount budgeted to study peculiarly male diseases. (The rest went to studying diseases afflicting both.)

Whereas in 1990 a woman suffering a heart attack had a better than even chance of being misdiagnosed or her dizziness or back pain dismissed or demoted, a woman in cardiac arrest now most likely will be diagnosed properly—and live to tell about it. According to the NIH, screening has resulted in a 40 percent decline in the incidence of and death from cervical cancer since 1970. And mortality from breast cancer dropped by 6 percent just between 1990 and 1994.

"Now we're going beyond screening, to improving management and treatment of diseases," Elena Rios, M.D., executive director of the National Hispanic Medical Association has said. "Women's health has moved beyond something people just talk about at the policy level."

Starting in the mid-1990s, the government required drug companies to include women in clinical trials. (Not long ago, the 155-pound white male was the norm for everything except obstetric and gynecologic concerns; even estrogen was tested initially exclusively on men.) Now women's body stats are figured in all tests to see how they experience well-being, disease, or pain; how medications metabolize differently in them; and how they manifest symptoms differently from men.

Some puzzle pieces are turning up. The Nurses' Health Study of more than 77,000 women conducted by Harvard University's School of Public Health, for example, unearthed the unusual finding that caffeine reduces Parkinson's risk in women who don't undergo hormone-replacement therapy (HRT) but jacks it right up in women who do subscribe to HRT. The NIH and Women's Health Initiative are studying thousands of postmenopausal women to learn about triggers and therapies to prevent osteoporosis and heart disease.

Drug companies, heeding the profit call, are rattling their test tubes for women-related therapies. According to the Pharmaceutical Research and Manufacturers of America, some 358 medicines to treat more than 30 diseases that disproportionately affect women (up from 263 in 1991) were in development in 2001. In addition, companies were working on 122 medicines for heart disease and stroke—which kill half a million women each year—and 68 medicines for lung cancer—the leading cancer killer of women.

Nor do the companies shy away from talking about them. On TV you are about as likely to see a commercial for heartburn remedy Nexium as for Nikes, Claritin as much as for Clairol, and Celebrex as much as for Celebrity Cruises. For the last few years, drug makers have pitched prescription products such as Zocor, Lipitor, and Allegra directly to consumers instead of just doctors. In one year, Merck spent more promoting Vioxx to consumers than PepsiCo spent advertising Pepsi.

"They have Viagra," says the woman in the ad. "Now we have Avlimil." The herbal "vita-vim" promises "an enhanced libido" and "more frequent and satisfying climaxes." In the ad for Eros Therapy's small, battery-operated soft-tipped vacuum pump (intended to improve blood flow), a sober 40-something woman tells the camera that "over 40 million women suffer from sexual dysfunction." More than a dozen American companies, including Pfizer, which makes

Viagra, and Procter & Gamble, are readying other "female sexual dys-function" aids from testosterone patches, to passion pills, to creams, gels, under-the-tongue drops, and nasal sprays, to electric clitoral-suction devices in a race to develop a women's equivalent to Viagra. Solving the problem for women is a lot harder than it is for men. A urologist's metallic box labeled "Male and Female Sexual Control Panel" suggests why. The one for men has a single on/off switch; the box for women is a complicated tangle of knobs, meters, and wires.

Women are also key players in the impotence solution sell. In 1998, Pfizer's sales and marketing prowess, coupled with the media frenzy, made Viagra such a household name that it was added to the *Oxford English Dictionary.* Nancy K. Bryan, Bayer Corporation's vice president for marketing for the new impotence treatment Levitra, believes that she knows how to get men to ask for help—and for Levitra. "We aim to communicate to men that it's a natural consequence of aging, like need-ing eyeglasses, and reach him through her. When it comes to sexual sat-isfaction, women play an important role for us," she says.

Levitra's U.K. Web site includes an extensive primer for women ("Honey, it's not you!") explaining what causes impotence and how best to broach the touchy subject. Its German Web site empathizes with women worried that their partner may no longer love them or may be having an affair. From pricey research, the Levitra team learned that consumers find Viagra's blue color too cool and medic-inal—so its pill is orange to express vibrancy and energy. (Its round shape and familiar Bayer logo are designed as reassurances.) And the company found that Viagra misstepped when it recruited Bob Dole as spokesman—stately and candid, yes, but it categorized erectile dys-function as an old man's ailment when the key audience is middle-aged.

Not long ago commercials for birth control drugs were taboo and the options limited. Now with the Ortho Evra patch, NuvaRing; the monthly injectable contraceptive, Lunelle; the Today sponge and its successors; and Plan B and Preven oral emergency contraceptives, "there have never been more options for women, in terms of tech-nologies," says Dr. David I. Kurss, medical director of the Women's

Wellness Center of Western New York. There has never been as much help conquering infertility or confirming a pregnancy either.

Hospitals are also preening for women's dollars, offering inducements from massage and laser therapies to mammograms and educational classes in their now ubiquitous women centers. Maternity wards across the country have become more like hotels, often advertising their amenities more than their medical care. It is not uncommon to drive away from a birthing center with a free car seat and baskets of baby supplies.

In 1995, Evanston Hospital began offering shoppers at Nordstrom's in nearby Wilmette, Illinois, a $40 discount on a $139 mammogram plus a free facial for having the mammogram right at the store in a less threatening, albeit admittedly unorthodox, setting. Pleased with the response, the hospital subsequently added screenings for bone density.

Women fear breast cancer more than any other illness, yet heart disease is their grimmest reaper. More women actually die of heart disease than do men. (Cancer is second.) A woman has a 1 in 8 chance of getting breast cancer in her lifetime and a 1 in 117 probability of getting cervical cancer. Stroke is the third biggest killer, taking down twice as many women each year as breast cancer. Women suffer half of all strokes—and 61 percent of the fatalities from it. Together, heart attack and stroke kill nearly twice as many American women as do all types of cancer combined.

Certain diseases seem to "favor" women. Some 75 percent of autoimmune diseases occur in women, as do 9 of 10 cases of lupus. Women suffer from rheumatoid arthritis two to three times more often than men, and half of women, versus 1 in 8 men over age 50, will have at least one osteoporosis-related fracture. Blame it on pregnancy, childbirth, menopause, and the structure of their urinary tract, but women experience incontinence twice as often as do men.

It is no wonder, then, that to sell Detrol La, Pharmacia Corporation worked to change the way incontinence sufferers view themselves. They renamed the condition "overactive bladder" and addressed it in a lighthearted, emphatic voice, making something that had been shameful, isolating, and embarrassing now approachable, human, and controllable.

Some "male conditions" also have migrated to the women's wards. Whereas women account for 28 percent of HIV cases reported since 1981, they are 32 percent of the more recent victims of the AIDS epidemic.

Fewer than 15 percent of people with anorexia, bulimia, or binge-eating disorder are male. Women are between five and eight times more likely than men to suffer from an over- or underactive thyroid. One in eight will develop a thyroid disorder during her lifetime. And nearly twice as many women (12 percent, or 12.4 million) are depressed. Women are also twice as likely to have panic disorder, post-traumatic stress disorder, generalized anxiety disorder, agoraphobia, and specific phobias, although about equal numbers of women and men have obsessive-compulsive disorder and social phobia.

Prozac had commandeered the women's market with its clarion call to return to yourself. Paxil gained traction by differentiating itself from Prozac as a remedy for anxiety, which can accompany depression, and emphasizing its specific benefits to combat restlessness, fatigue, difficulty concentrating, muscle tension, and disturbed sleep.

Women are also the driving force behind elective plastic surgery. The most common elected surgeries are eyelid and nose repairs, according to the American Academy of Facial Plastic and Reconstructive Surgery. Botox injection is the most common nonsurgical procedure. There are even Botox parties, where friends congregate for camaraderie and wrinkle relief.

Looking to horn in on the runaway Botox train, medical entrepreneurs have come up with other techniques and cosmetic fillers to smooth out a furrow, correct hollowness around the eyes, add fullness to thin lips, and banish laugh lines. Collagen is branded as Zyderm and Zyplast. The FDA recently approved Restylane and Perlane. Artes Medical's Artefill forces the body to form new tissue that fills in wrinkles. Women are even using stretch mark–reducing emulsion StriVectin-SD on their faces.

Health maintenance organizations (HMOs) are also preening for women who overwhelmingly pick the family's health plan, even if their husband's company pays for it. Several now allow women to visit their gynecologist or to get their annual mammogram without requiring their primary care physician's "permission." D.C. Chartered Health Plan gave new members Thanksgiving and Christmas baskets and offered prospects free health club memberships and pagers. In the November enrollment period, when 60 to 70 percent of its membership is up for renewal, HIP Health Plans hands out a free prepaid long-distance phone card to anyone requesting information. "Health care has learned a lot from our cousins in retailing," says Allan R. Glick, senior vice president for marketing at HIP.

Female pioneers of prevention have turned natural care remedies into a $4 billion-a-year industry and pumped up sales of olive oil, soy, red wine, grape juice, green tea, and St. John's wort—whatever research identifies as the latest golden apple. (Barred by the FDA from touting supposed benefits, many companies dance around regulations. For example, Well Quest International calls its Bloussant herbal bust enhancer "nature's answer to a more beautiful bust line" and claims that 84 percent of users grow between one-half and two cup sizes. However, its ads are carefully worded to not say that the product *increases* breast size but rather enhances it.)

Women also have led the pilgrimage to acupuncturists, chiropractors, massage therapists, and other alternatives to conventional Western medicine. And they have blazed the trail on vitamin consumption. Recently, cosmetics giant Avon has branched out to sell vitamins, weight-control programs, and other "wellness" merchandise. Olay has extended its line to Beauty Nutrients and Wellness Nutrients vitamins. And Revlon launched a vitamin line for nails, skin, and hair.

When It Comes to Health Care . . .

- Women will change doctors faster than men if dissatisfied with their health care, and they are more likely

> to be dissatisfied and frustrated with the way doctors talk to them.
> - Word of mouth is the most important source of health information and referral for women, with their doctors and nurses as secondary sources.
> - Women want an intimate relationship with their health care providers, someone who sees the whole person with a complex life, not just lesions and lab values, says Cynthia Gorney, associate dean at the Graduate School of Journalism at the University of California at Berkeley.

Although their motivation is more marketing than medical, companies have formulated gender-specific products and lines. Bayer Women's Aspirin Plus Calcium lessens cardiac risk and improves bone health. Clif's Luna bars contain calcium, folic acid and other B vitamins, iron, and soy, but at only 180 calories they are much less fattening than typical energy bars. Nutrient waters contain fiber, vitamin C, calcium, soy, and selenium, and Twinlab concocted Energy Fuel, the first energy drink for women. There are new Women's Tylenol Menstrual Relief and Quaker Oatmeal Nutrition for Women. Men rarely develop cellulite, but women will spend treasuries on skin-firming lotions that promise to get rid of it. GNC, CVS, Nature's Bounty, Biotech, Natrol, and One-A-Day all have lines designed for women.

Some companies have crafted ads that cater to women's desire for control. This drive is so strong that the NIH claims that it is harder for women to stop smoking because they like the feeling of control associated with cigarettes. Excedrin used no graphics to illustrate how fast it works, close-ups of faces in pain, or testimonials of newfound relief. Instead, a spot for its new no-water-needed QuickTabs showed a feuding couple at a restaurant. The woman takes a pill from her purse, pops it in her mouth, and tosses her glass of water into her date's face. "New Excedrin QuickTabs melt in your mouth fast for headache relief so you can save your water for other things," says the voiceover. Then her date's weak response: "I didn't know she was your sister." Bozell Executive Creative Director Tony Granger says, "We needed to get away from packaged-goods formula of benefit-drive, annoying mnemonic, or a little graphic of penetrating heat."

Accounting for 70 percent of their customers, women are the lifeblood of pharmacies. No mere messengers, these. Rather than assume doctor knows best, female patrons are largely making up their own minds—and diagnoses. Their keen interest in "wellness" products and services has prompted many chains to move beyond simple blood pressure screenings. Giant Stores of Landover, Maryland, for example, provides immunizations and consultations on ailments under a "Relax, Renew, Revive" banner.

Drugstores have mutated from pill dispensers to problem solvers. "Pharmacy drives our business and is our lifeblood," says Eckerd Corporation CEO Wayne Harris. But Eckerd is greatly expanding the cosmetics offerings in its new uber-sized stores, where the "flex" pharmacy uses robotics and pill-counting technology.

An entire industry of pharmaceutical dot-coms—from Drugstore.com to PlanetRx.com—has joined "name brand" pharmacies such as CVS and Rite Aid in wooing women online. Their appeal— time-saving help and money-back security.

In addition to changing the way medicine is taught, what's changed is whom it's being taught to. In her classroom at the medical school of the University of California–San Francisco, Rachel K. Sobel says, "the young, white, male biochemistry whiz—the traditional student of times past—would look like an underrepresented minority" amid all the women. Women constitute 57 percent of her class and close to 50 percent of the national average. And droves are heading into traditional male specialties such as surgery.

Some gender inequities in medical research and treatment still linger. For example, reproductive health problems are among the least reimbursed by insurers.

Hysterectomies are routine, albeit often unwarranted, according to the American College of Obstetricians and Gynecologists. Around 600,000 are performed in the United States each year because

HMOs cover them and they are the most expeditious way to deal with fibroids. And overall, women get less thorough evaluations than men for similar complaints, the Commonwealth Fund found. However, as more women wear the white coats and call the shots, this will fade in memory, like dying in childbirth.

For women, "take care" isn't just an empty salutation: Whether by default, nurture, or nature it's one of their prime responsibilities—and expenses.

7

Travel: Comfort, Cleanliness, and a Good Hair Dryer

Dog biscuits and disposable bathing suits didn't work as amenities in Westin Hotel rooms. Neither did balls for children (too much potential for noise and damage), soap dispensers in showers (individually wrapped soap is preferred), or scales in bathrooms (who wants to be reminded of their weight on vacation?).

However, guest response to an 1875-watt hair dryer was enthusiastic enough to make that a room mainstay. Ditto Starbucks coffee, hookups for laptops, luxurious shampoos, heavenly beds, and heavenly baths with dual showerheads for more powerful sprays.

Sue A. Brush, senior vice president for Westin's parent, Starwood Hotels & Resorts Worldwide, considers dozens of new ideas each year to upgrade the 75 products that go into each Westin room in North America. Her mission is to find what guests want—enough to pay for it.

A few years ago, in its first national ad campaign ever, Westin showed a power girl who "drives a hard bargain, drives sales through the roof, and drives a three-liter turbo-charged car" and wondered aloud "who's she sleeping with?" More recently, the chain's surveys found that what guests most want from a hotel room is a good night's sleep. Out went the lumpy pillows, floral-quilted bedspreads, and meager-thread-count sheets. In went heavenly beds and ads showing models sensuously sleeping in them. (Westin held a contest to select the best mattresses and pillows.) Next came the heavenly bath, and soon after, divine fitness centers.

Men may wind up footing the bill, but it's women who primarily make the vacation plans. (RoperASW found that women do so in 88 percent of couples and, presumably, 100 percent of single women's households.) As a rule, women are more receptive to the happiness and/or adventure a rental car offers rather than someone vaulting through airports for a speedier checkout. And women are more inclined to empathize with someone indulging at a spa rather than staring at a deserted beach. Before terrorism and a weak economy forced the industry into a ditch, Alamo Rent-a-Car had scrapped promoting unlimited mileage to stress its unlimited "smileage." Similarly, instead of showing pools, beaches, lobbies, and dancing bellmen, most hotel ads show guests reveling in the activities and atmosphere.

Other way stations have taken to attracting women through their children. Holiday Inn lets kids eat free. A mom who is also a CPA calculates how much her family saved enjoying Days Inn's complimentary buffet breakfast—and how many calories the family spent playing in the motel's pool. Howard Johnson wages that its peewee guests have more fun than those at pricier rivals. In one ad, kids in a Howard Johnson pool have a blast, while those at a snobbier inn bum at poolside after a waiter confiscates their water toys.

Women have long steered leisure travel; now they are on par with men as expense-account road warriors. In 1970, just around 1 percent of business travelers were female; today they take up half the bulkheads, according to Westin.

Sheraton Hotels & Resorts aimed for women in a print ad in which a child implores, "Please press our mom's suit; she had to fly coach." Another child's pleas in that campaign include, "Make sure my mother gets her faxes, especially the one with my math homework." Such advertising is aimed for the heart, not the head, of the business traveler.

For two years Embassy Suites puffed about the functionality of its large two-room suites. In 2003 it went a step further—showing the freeing effect of that space on its guests' psyches compared with travelers who stay in cramped, boxy hotel rooms. A businesswoman, crouched inside a clear acrylic box, makes a dispirited presentation.

Women travelers have—quite literally—brought hotels out of the Dark Ages. Their growing presence has banished the dark wood, dark marble, and dark corners of the clublike lounges of hotels past, replaced by lighter lobbies and tighter security, bright fitness rooms, and unisex "wellness" centers.

Starwood Hotels & Resorts Worldwide designed its W Hotels, which opened in 2000, for women. There is no dark wood or leather-clad lounge that telegraphs manliness, but there are lots of full-length mirrors and mirrors with magnifiers, as well as good bathroom lighting by which to apply makeup, says Juergen Bartels, previously chairman and chief executive officer of Westin Hotels Resorts and now CEO of Le Meridien Hotel Group. Each room has a hair dryer and iron, all-natural-fiber furnishings, and sumptuous baths.

Sheraton has beefed up the lighting in its parking lots and promises to not give women a ground floor room if there's a vacancy elsewhere. Hyatt has upgraded its bathroom illumination and toiletries, replaced wooden hangers with padded ones, and added low-cal dishes to its round-the-clock room service and a quick-turn-around laundry.

Embassy Suites realized that many normally extroverted women become introverted on the road, so it made its public areas "wide open with soaring atriums. This is more comfortable for women than going into closed cocktail lounge or breakfast room," says Senior Vice President Mark A. Synder.

Inter-Continental and Crowne Plaza Hotels & Resorts enhanced the healthy choices on its menus and the quality of its in-room security and terrycloth robes. "We've evaluated all our marketing materials to ensure [that] women are presented in positive, professional roles," noted Robert Mayer, vice president for marketing at Crowne.

Feedback from its Women's Business Travel Advisory Board prompted Wyndham Hotels to add a library in its garden hotel lobbies as a social alternative to a bar. The chain routinely calls guests five minutes before room service arrives to avoid unpleasant surprises.

While airlines haven't adjusted their seat lumbar support to form fit a female silhouette, some have added legroom and revamped their premium-class meal service. Women were not the impetus for British Airways' first-class sleeper seats that recline to fully horizontal beds, but their comfort and partitions for privacy appeal to many women.

Delta recently launched the new airline Song to serenade women. "No airline has targeted women before, but that's where we're aiming," said John Selvaggio, president of Song. "Women buy 75 percent of American leisure travel tickets and 90 percent of family travel tickets. They're discriminating and know a good value when they see it." (Selvaggio expects women to see it in Song's low prices and high quality, with digital TV and music at every seat and baby changing stations in every lavatory.) "In my experience, where women go, men follow," he said.

Because women are using limousines more, limousine companies have responded by becoming "more like luxury hotels on wheels," said Tom Mazza, executive director of the National Limousine Association. "Men want to get to their destination as quickly as possible, and they care about the model and year of the car. Women view the car as a safe haven to close their eyes and are more concerned that drivers dress immaculately and speak well." Thus the car service companies have become much more careful about hiring and are investing more in driver safety and training programs. Drivers are trained to "do little extras" like storing a coat for a client until she returns from a trip, picking up her groceries, or even baby-sitting, he says.

To appeal to women who represent the majority of adventure travelers, the cruise industry has reinvented itself. Now it is a portal to action and excitement instead of a sedentary, regimented variety-show-and-buffet vacation. In one Royal Caribbean ad, a family rides wave runners and swims with stingrays off Grand Cayman while a woman's voice urges them to "Get out there."

Women also have presaged the changed look of luggage (they buy two-thirds of it). Suitcases with wheels are commonplace now, says Robert Ermatinger, executive director of the Luggage & Leather Goods Manufacturers of America, but this innovation was born to make them more portable for women.

Different Strokes for Different Genders

Wyndham Hotels discovered that women travelers care, above all else, about good service when they choose a hotel. For men, it is location. More than complimentary liquor or flowers, what wins women's loyalty is the small gesture that acknowledges them as individuals.

Women also appreciate a deep tub—not just a shower stall. Eighty-two percent of female guests at London's Halkin Hotel preferred baths to showers, whereas just 14 percent of the men soaked their cares away in tubs.

Natania Janz, a London-based psychologist and coeditor of *Women Travel,* says that women on the road look for meaningful contact, whereas men tend to stand back in detachment, snapping pictures. This explains why women like to shop, she believes. It is not a matter of acquisitiveness only, but a way to "get into a foreign culture and engage."

A 1997 survey from the Novotel New York Hotel staff found that male guests keep the cleanest bedrooms and that women are likeliest to pocket free toiletries.

Luggage, airline seats, hotel lobbies, security, and amenities— all have recognized that the woman who makes the family's vacation plans is just as likely as a man to be a business road warrior.

8

Hope in a Jar:
The Beauty Biz

In the Dark Ages, noble ladies swigged arsenic and smeared bats' blood on their faces to better their complexions. Pioneer women patted on the warm urine of young boys to fade their freckles. And in Victorian England, the desire for a Scarlett O'Hara waist was so fierce that women had ribs removed to acquire one. Earlier feminists saw makeup as the means to write their own story, independent of their husband's or father's plans.

The yearning to be beautiful is not new. Today, even as women claim that inner beauty is what counts, they still spend inordinate time, effort, and money on looking younger, thinner, and better. Americans spend more each year on beauty than they do on education. For cosmetics alone, Taylor Nelson Sofres estimates, each American woman shells out, on average, over $154 a year.

This outlay is expected to increase. Goldman Sachs figures that the $24 billion global beauty industry is growing at more than twice the rate of the developed world's gross domestic product (GDP), a result of affluent aging baby boomers and lots more discretionary income in the West and growing middle classes in developing countries. Brazil has more "Avon ladies" than it has men and women in its army and navy.

More than 9 out of 10 American women regularly wear makeup. As a woman's income rises, generally so does her use of beauty products. Makeup seems aptly named: Whether used to highlight features or cover them up, most women say that makeup makes them feel *up*, better, more confident. But this does not mean that they fall for whatever promise or fantasy is being hawked.

Promise is the lifeblood of the bewitching beauty biz. Once, Rubinstein, Arden, and Max Factor used various degrees of "fear of looking ugly" and "pleasure of looking beautiful" to sell powder. Selling to today's jaded consumers requires more sophisticated nuances. Brands subtly tap into something bigger, less tangential than the product itself. Revlon founder Charles Revson knew that he wasn't selling lipstick; he was selling hope. Estée Lauder, whose marketing budget is more than 20 times the size of its research and development (R&D) budget, has turned an arsenal of creams and lotions into women's intimate friends.

We now believe that makeup can do for us what a paint job does to a house—give it a new lease on life. Women who can just as easily buy a $5 brand of drugstore lipstick or use Crisco on their face plunk down $55 for a tube of Cle Peau. It is more than the rosewater scent or the way it swivels or the feel of the hefty container; it is the fantasy suggested and empowerment delivered.

Of course, it's a given that the product works—and works better than anything available yesterday. Cosmetic companies constantly search for the new and improved—instant-drying nail polish, smudgeless eye liner, facial cloths impregnated with cleansers, transdermal vitamin C patches, St. John's wort lipstick from Tony & Tina, and "Touch Me Then Try to Leave" cream from Bene-fit.

Wrinkle filler Restylane may replace Botox because it is longer lasting. Hard Candy launched a pastel lacquer crusade. The "naturals" market, begun with The Body Shop, grew to include green tea, fruit extracts such as the Fructis hair care products, "aqua" marine water, and spas, salons, and clubs with an emphasis on being fit—not just thin. Philosophy skin care products come with a self-help homily, and exfoliating foot cream Soul Owner comes with an exhortation to "review your only true assets. You own your values, your integrity."

Shiseido and Avon claim that their Body Creator skin gel and Cellu-Sculpt cream, respectively, can melt away body fat. New Olay Regenerist "revolutionary cell care" was developed for those "not ready for a cosmetic procedure." L'Oreal launches three to four new products a year—three times what it did a decade ago. *Antiaging* and *well-being* continue to be magic words, admits Carol Hamilton, L'Oreal senior vice president.

So are *whitening* and *women-specific.* Half the households in America bought a toothpaste with whitener last year. Today, "women want products specifically for themselves, yet toothpaste was one of the few personal care categories with no products specifically for them," said Diane Dietz, marketing director for Crest Rejuvenating Effects. Based on feedback from toothpaste-tasting parties, Procter & Gamble imbued the glimmering aqua paste with subtle vanilla and cinnamon flavoring and a compound to produce a gentle tingling sensation to provide a "sensory signal" of gum health and fresh breath, put it in a matching teal tube and pearlescent box, and promised it would "remineralize, revitalize and restore whiteness." (Procter & Gamble admits that it doesn't do much more than other Crest products, but users think they are having "a better brushing experience.")

Following the bread crumb trail, many companies are designing new products for women over age 40, who buy more cosmetics than the generation after them and willingly pay a premium for what they like. Pond's Institute, L'Oreal's Plentitude, and Procter & Gamble's Oil of Olay Provital cater to drying skin. "With 30 years of makeup experience, these women are hard to fool," says Mark Schar, general manager of skin care at Procter & Gamble. "They don't relate to the classic beauty model with the 1000-yard stare; they look for inner warmth and connection" and for proof that their skin can be reenergized. At the opposite end of the spectrum, in late 2003 Avon launched Mark, a cosmetic line for 16- to 24-year-old women.

The bread crumbs also have led marketers to consider not just the potential size of their collective audience but also their individual sizes and weights. Tampax's Always Maximum Protection now comes in a pad that is 30 percent larger to accommodate women sized 14 and up. Previously, pads were designed for size 6 women and were advertised showing women trying to attract muscular bare-chested men. More recent ads feature plus-size models and focus on the tampon wearer's comfort and cleanliness.

Sometimes the "weight" is emotional. Hair is a *heavily* emotional subject. According to Procter & Gamble, 77 percent of women admit that a bad hair day means a bad day overall—that how their hair looks is a key indicator to how they feel. Dove tried to make some hair-raising news with its "weightless" shampoo and conditioners that won't mat hair down. And Pantene's Daily Moisture Renewal shampoo and conditioner in one was designed to salve dry or damaged hair.

Years ago, in the "Does she or doesn't she" days (defined by Clairol's signature advertising), whether a woman colored her hair was a guarded secret. Now, says New York colorist to the stars Brad Johns, "people see hair color as a cosmetic, and everybody's coloring it." According to L'Oreal, nearly 60 percent of American women (up from 40 percent in 1976) regularly bleach, streak, tone, skunk, or strand their hair, sometimes with colors so unnatural that it is clearly not just their hairdressers who know for sure. L'Oreal's signature "Because I'm worth it" line, first run in 1973, helped it surpass Clairol and define how a new generation honored themselves rather than furtively sneaking around.

Scent is another emotional heavyweight. American women use more aromatic, moisturizing, special treatment soaps and lotions than any other culture or time in history. Women, whom research shows have a keener sense of smell than men, lead the olfactory charge. Banish the image of men wrapping up Des Lys by Annick Goutal or Dolly Girl by Anna Sui for their lady loves at Christmas; year round it is women who buy 99 percent of their own fragrances and 60 percent of what men wear, says Camille McDonald, president and CEO of Givenchy, Inc.

In Bloomingdale's Manhattan flagship store, nicknamed "Stink Alley," well-groomed spritzers accost passersby with scent samples, but not always via spray. Shoppers disliked this, so Lauder "beauty guides" offer a hand massage with Black Cashmere lotion, spray their own wrists and let customers sniff, or hand out scent cards.

A decade ago women wore perfume primarily to relate to others. Now its prime purpose is to express oneself, says Fragrance Foundation Director Annette Green. Perfume, she says, has followed the women's movement, moving "from glamour and seduction to pampering and managing our mind and bodies and strengthening our identity."

Cosmetic companies are also changing the way cosmetics are sold. To encourage women to buy more on impulse, Lauder replaced glass counters in stores with open displays that let women browse, touch, and test without having to ask for help. Avon opened boutique kiosks at malls to reach the millions of women not home during the day. And Sephora lets customers play in the aisles. "Young women loathe waiting at the cosmetics counter, having to get someone's attention," says Charla Krupp, an editor at *Glamour*. They prefer to grab a lipstick at Victoria's Secret or a boutique store or to shop online. Dozens of cosmetics Web sites have been launched, including Sears' T.I.M.E. (The Instant Makeup Expert).

The beauty quest propels women to reconstruct their faces and bodies with surgery or "cutless" procedures. The economy may have stalled, but in 2002 nearly 7 million Americans—88 percent of them women—spent $7.7 billion on cosmetic procedures such as liposuction, breast augmentation, eyelid surgery, nose reconstruction, and breast reduction, according to the American Society for Aesthetic Plastic Surgery. They spent millions more on fat, collagen, and Botox injections, skin peels, laser hair removal, and "designer dentistry."

Women today "go to the dermatologist like our mothers went to the hairdresser," says Pamela Baxter, president of Estée Lauder's Specialty Group. Its Clinique touts that it was developed by dermatologist Dr. Norman Orentreich, and it recently signed Dr. Karen Grossman to endorse Prescriptives' Dermapolish, an at-home skin peel.

Medical experts reassure women about beauty products; so do famous faces. L'Oreal has Sarah Jessica Parker for sassy Garnier hair color, and Revlon LipGlide Color Gloss lipstick has Halle Berry, Salma Hayek, Lucy Liu, and Rachel Weisz. Rock chick Elizabeth Jagger struts for Lancome, along with models Devon Aoki, Oluchi, and

Uma Thurman for Miracle fragrance. Catherine Zeta-Jones is the face for Arden; Penelope Cruz represents Ralph Lauren Fragrances' Glamorous.

In 2003, Liya Kebede joined Elizabeth Hurley and Carolyn Murphy as the face of Estée Lauder. The reedlike 24-year-old Ethiopian with café-au-lait skin was the first black woman to represent the brand in Lauder's history. This was no accident but a deliberate effort to reach a wider audience: African-Americans account for 19 percent of all cosmetic sales. A *New York Times* survey found that from 1998 to 2002, fashion magazine covers nearly doubled their use of non-white subjects.

With neither a celebrity nor a white-coat endorsement, grooming aids have attracted loyalists by zigging while others zagged. Altoids plays up that its flavors are "curiously strong" with edgy ads that emphasize attitude to appeal to urban sophisticates. Listerine Pocket Paks take a different tack, pushing that they kill germs, not just bad breath, said Wes Pringle, group marketing director for oral care at Pfizer.

Companies that previously catered exclusively to men have turned their gaze to the fairer sex. For years, guys got all the sympathy for hair loss, whereas women with thinning hair and bald patches suffered silently—and secretly tried every possible remedy. Then Rogaine put essentially the same 2 percent minoxidil solution in a salmon-colored box instead of its usual blue one and began courting women. (In one ad, one sister confides her hair loss trauma to the other.) Women now account for 30 percent of Rogaine's sales.

Gillette Company had become synonymous with shaving by addressing men. A decade ago it turned its attention to woman. As shavers, they outnumber men in the United States by 20 percent, and they shave an area, on average, nine times larger than what men do. However, Gillette soon learned that the rules that it had long lived by did not apply.

Men view shaving as a skill; women see it as a chore. Men think that the longer they use a blade, the likelier it is to nick them. Women think just the opposite. When a man cuts himself shaving, he blames the razor; a woman blames herself. Men spend more on shaving gear than on any other type of toiletry; women spend a fraction on shaving products compared with other personal care stuff. "While men describe the ideal shaving product in terms of benefits, women describe negative things they want to avoid," said John Darman, North Atlantic Group vice president of blades and razors. Yet both willingly accepted Gillette as an authority on shaving.

At first, Gillette tried to sell women a man's razor colored pink. No response. Then in 1992 it redesigned its Sensor Excel shaver (and marketing) and has continued to study how and where women shave to accommodate them. Gillette for Women Venus, for example, has an oval-shaped cartridge, ergonomic handle, and storage compact "to convey a balance of femininity, confidence, and strength to resonate with women worldwide," said Mary Ann Pesce, vice president of Global Business Management. (In 2003, Schick spent a queen's ransom—$120 million—promoting a new three-bladed razor for women called Intuition. The company embedded examples of "women's intuition" in 13 episodes of the All American Girl TV show.)

Beauty Statistics

- The average woman owns 6.1 tubes of lipstick.
- Fifty-eight percent of women polish their nails regularly (although just 2 percent regularly go to a salon for a professional manicure).
- A third of women get facials.
- Nine percent of women have already had cosmetic surgery.
- Eighty-two percent of women say that they *could* live without mascara or blush—but don't want to.

Women's passion to look good has remained steadfast through the years, but just as the definition of beauty has become more encompassing, so have the dollars devoted to it.

9

Dressed to Thrill

Women have a love-hate relationship with clothes. Following food, it is the top reason that women shop, and they spend more on their wardrobes than anything, save food, investments, and vacations, says Leo Shapiro, of the Chicago-based Leo J. Shapiro & Associates consultancy.

No surprise, women buy virtually all their own clothes. Perhaps less obviously, they also buy most of what their kids wear *and* 46 percent of what their guys wear. They "influence" the purchase of much more, according to Cotton, Inc. A study conducted by the Wirthlin Group found that, on average, women outnumber men in men's departments by three to one.

It's not that women are "slaves to fashion" so much as that their own size changes. Most women have four different-sized clothes in their closets for different times of the month. Yet most apparel purchases are propelled by *want* more than need. Women buy clothes because they enjoy doing so. Four of five women say that it makes them happy.

At least as much as a car, home, or job and perhaps more than anything, clothes are a statement of a woman's identity—how she sees herself and how she wants others to see her. Picking Saint John or Calvin Klein, Ann Taylor or Tommy Hilfiger, Donna Karan or Diesel, a woman defines herself as traditional or trendy, chaste, nature girl, or seductress.

The basic premise of retailing has long been "Give the lady what she wants." Increasingly, now that casual Fridays have become casual everyday, women want comfort and informality—pushing suits, pointy bras, and dry-clean-only garments to the back of the bin. (According to the NPD Group, 58 percent of women note laundering instructions before buying a garment, nearly half have washed a garment with a "Dry Clean Only" label, and 82 percent of all apparel units now bought are machine washable.) And it's goodbye to the click, click, click of heels: 49 percent of women almost always wear flats.

Did You Know?

- Shoes are one of the most purchased items on the Internet.
- The average bra size has gone from a 34B to a 36C in recent years.
- Seven of 10 Americans pick jeans as their first choice for casual wear. During periods of uncertainty, women gravitate to the utterly reliable tried-and-true uniform—jeans, sneakers, and a white shirt—says Ginger Reeder, a spokeswoman for Neiman Marcus.
- The little black dress first popularized by designer Coco Chanel in 1926 is in as many closets as jeans.
- About 30 percent of apparel bought online is sent back—twice the amount bought at conventional stores—according to the Gartner Group research firm.
- Forty-six percent of women who see something they like on a friend will try to find something similar, with younger consumers feeling even more strongly, according to Cotton, Inc.

Designers and retailers are offering more plus sizes to reflect our real shape. According to Cotton, Inc., 53 percent of American women wear a size 12 or larger, and spending in this sector grew four times what it did in smaller sizes from 1998 to 2001. (Even *Vogue*—the arbiter of taste and stanchion of thin—devoted a whole issue to larger women in the spring of 2002.) Because super-sized has become normal-sized in apparel just as in soda, full-figured women, as they are now called to soothe ruffled feathers, rarely shop in separate sections as they had to not long ago. "Women want to shop together. A size 18 or 24 doesn't want to be sequestered in another area," says Emme, a large-sized model whose True Beauty by Emme apparel line is sold in JC Penney. (It has joined now-crowded racks stocked with Queen Latifah's Curvation lingerie; Tommy Hilfiger, Eddie Bauer, and Sara Lee's Just My Size casual clothes; and Fruit of the Loom's Fit for Me lingerie, among others.)

While the average fashion model today is 35 pounds lighter and 4 inches taller than the average woman, larger models are showing up more and more. Aida Brigman, director of the Plus Division at Click, says that in 3 years the number of larger models the agency represents has tripled.

Still, some stores and designers play sizing games to skirt the "psychological barrier" a certain size presents, says Judith Russell, executive editor of "The Apparel Strategist," a trade newsletter. Chico's, for example, has its own size scheme of 0 to 3 (3 corresponds to the standard size 14 to 16). "A woman's not going to want to leave Chico's and become a size 16 when at Chico's she's a size 3," says Russell.

You may need a size 14 pattern when you usually buy a size 10 dress because the pattern industry doesn't cheat. It adheres to a time-honored standard, not the vanity sizing many designers and retailers have adopted. The higher the price tag on the clothes, the smaller the sizes must read, the better and more confident a woman feels wearing them, and the more devoted to the store or designer she becomes. Who doesn't want to flaunt a teeny size or imagine wearing a dress with the label sticking out bowling-shoe style so that others can wince in jealousy?

Why do women who can buy a simple white T-shirt for $12 pay $120 for an almost identical one? Marketers know that it can instill a feeling of power in the wearer, so they spend heavily to inspire confidence in their logo or label.

In both food and fashion, it looks like such marketers are losing the battle. Private-label or store brands now make up 36 percent of total apparel sales, according to NPD Group, up from 26 percent from 1998. And more women now pride themselves on how little, not how much, they paid. Target pioneered the concept of "discount chic." T. J. Maxx made the point in its "Some people get it. Some people get it for less" ads, and Payless is singing this tune with an assist from Star Jones, self-proclaimed "Diva of Stylish Shoes," and its "Look smart. Payless" theme.

Seven of 10 women say that they only buy clothes on sale. Two of three wait for the midseason sales. Ninety-one percent claim that they walk away from those soft-as-butter Capris if they can't justify the price. And on the rare occasion that they do pay full price, 9 of 10 women suspect that they have overpaid.

Once a woman finds a shift or shirt that she likes, she is intensely loyal. A Madison Avenue shoe boutique knows this: A sign in its window reads, "If the shoe fits, buy it in every color." Minnesota-based women's wear retailer Christopher & Banks Corporation has won shoppers' loyalty (and commerce) without benefit of a catalog or online purchasing capability. What it does have are racks of polyester jumpers and flowered cardigans, lots of gingham and embroidery, and a thorough and profound knowledge of its customer, down to whether she prefers a tuna salad sandwich or chunks of tuna on her salad. She's a 48-year-old suburban mother of two who could be a teacher, nurse, or bank teller; who drives a minivan and whose husband drives a Jeep; who prefers TGIF to McDonald's; who reads *People* and *Good Housekeeping* but not *Vogue*; and who "doesn't want to shop where her children do," says Joseph Pennington, president of the company. She wants to look her age but not aged, and she wants matching clothes, nothing that screams sexy or youthful.

Stores are also grouping clothes so that women can buy outfits rather than prowl several departments for matches. More stores are offering personal shoppers who assemble collections in try-on rooms. (Some online retailers allow women to "try on" clothing via a virtual model.) And the try-on rooms themselves have changed. Many rival Manhattan studio apartments in size and amenities.

Still, for 37 percent of women, shopping for clothes is often maddening. The average women struggles into 10 pairs of jeans before connecting with the one that fits best, according to Lee Jeans. And a survey for zipdisk maker Iomega Corporation concluded that women find buying a bathing suit just a shade less stressful than facing a hard-drive failure.

Indeed, shopping for a swimsuit—facing your nearly naked reflection in a dressing-room mirror—can be traumatic. Research indicates that women try on an average of 15 bathing suits before buying one.

Shopping for frumpy and tentlike maternity clothes used to be dispiriting. Now, with boot-cut pants, fitted button-down blouses, and denim skirts with drawstrings, it's time to flaunt that bulge. Maternity clothes are so cool that some moms have them altered to wear after delivery.

Even more *fun* to shop for is lingerie. Frederick's of Hollywood's see-through nighties trimmed with marabou feathers and scarlet French maid costumes were once risqué and revolutionary. Nowadays, Victoria's Secret has made sexy lingerie as mainstream as cotton underwear, said Dorothy Lakner, an analyst with CIBC World Markets. (Victoria's Secret also does flannel, she says, because women want snuggly as well as sexy.)

Take the thong, which may have been launched on its road to superstardom by Monica Lewinsky one mid-November afternoon in 1995. Since then it has gone from a footnote in the Starr Report to a staple in women's wardrobes. More than 120 million thongs were sold in the United States in a recent year, according to NPD Group.

And not just at Victoria's Secret and Frederick's but also at prurient Wal-Mart and for women of all dimensions. Just My Size sells thongs to fit 64-inch hips. There are even maternity thongs.

Maidenform's Moment

For decades, Maidenform led the industry it spawned by posing models in surrealistic dreamscape fantasizing what they could accomplish in their bras. In 1949, "I Dreamed I Went Shopping in My Maidenform Bra" was the first enactment. In subsequent spots women dreamed they floated down the Nile on a barge, swayed the jury, rode a merry-go-round, and tamed lions in their Maidenforms.

The ads brought then-unmentionable lingerie into the limelight and made Maidenform the generic word for bra. After 20 years, the campaign was mothballed—young women associated it with their mothers, traditionalism, and confinement—but 11 years later, in 1979, the dreamer reappeared, half-clothed in "You Never Know Where She'll Turn Up" ads. She (and her sisters) turned up at the theater, practicing law, disembarking from a helicopter carrying a briefcase, walking a tightrope between the tops of the Chrysler and Empire State buildings, and practicing medicine in their Maidenforms.

The company tried different approaches, including featuring famous handsome men ruminating about lingerie, in ads that never showed bras—or their wearers. "When a woman wears beautiful lingerie, it says she likes herself," British actor Michael York mused. "I think that's sexy." Omar Sharif explained, "Lingerie says a lot about a woman. . . . I listen as often as possible." However, women grumbled about the implication—that they bought underwear just to please men—and in 1991 Maidenform took a more PC feminist stance. New ads parodied female stereotypes such as a chick, a doll, a tomato, and a fox and showed women in old-fashioned panniers, bustles, and corsets. "Isn't it nice to live in a time when women aren't being pushed around so much anymore?" it asked, poking fun at clichés about women and positioning itself as a company that sees beyond stereotypes.

Despite its out-there marketing, though, Maidenform got clobbered in the marketplace. Once, the theory went, women found a bra that fit right, they would stay with it. This is not true anymore, a casualty of in-store price promotions from such stalwarts as Sara Lee, Warnaco Group, and VF Corp and the designer brands.

Fashion marketers are recognizing that women don't dress to thrill as much as they dress to identify themselves—to declare how they see themselves and how they want others to see them. As for buying the rest of the family's clothes? It has a lot to do with how she sees them (or wants to see them) and how she wants *others* to see them.

10

Someone's in the Kitchen with Dinah

Whoever said you are what you eat had no clue how twenty-first-century Americans would take this admonition to heart. We've got a slew of demands: We want less trans-fat and fewer carbs and more nutrition and antioxidants, yet at the table we are Jekyll-and-Hyde duplicitous, scarfing down Devil Dogs and double-beef patties with a devil-may-care attitude.

Fare that is convenient—ready-to-eat or heat-and-eat, preferably without utensils—tops our "most wanted" list—as long as it is delicious, according to the Institute of Food Technologists. Healthy foods or avoiding those evil temptresses loaded with fats and calories comes second, explaining why so many labels promise "no," "low," "less than," or "reduced." More than 70 percent of shoppers regularly read the label for nutritional content. Yet how we eat often depends on whether the meal has any social component or is merely a fuel stop.

Food marketers have long known who's "womanning" the stove; now they are adjusting to the fact that she'd rather not. (Some view kitchens as museum artifacts and recommend storing important papers in the oven, where a fire is unlikely.) Thus marketers are cooking up "speed scratch" meals (Green Giant Create a Meal frozen veggies) and shortcuts (Oscar Mayer's precooked bacon) to help shrink-wrap meal-prep time to the current 15-minute "threshold of acceptability." In the 1960s, dinners took on average 1.5 hours to make. Prep time is condensing because 77 percent of all dinners in America are prepared by women, said Harry Balzer, vice president of NPD Group. "With all the demands and pressures on their time, cooking is a job they want to get out of, and that's transforming meal preparation."

In more than three of four households, women are the primary food shoppers too, and they have shaved the time they spend there to an average of 24 minutes a visit, down 25 percent from 5 years ago. When men go, they often tote a list their female partner wrote. Still, 92 percent of women use coupons, according to coupon clearinghouse NCH. And most shoppers want to be able to bank, fill prescriptions, rent videos, and drop off dry cleaning at their superstore.

Today, "cooks" are more food assemblers than preparers. Half of all main meals consist of just one dish, according to the Food Marketing Institute. Fewer than one in four meals prepared at home use more than one appliance (down from nearly 40 percent in 1990), and only 38 percent include *anything* made from scratch, according to the Grocery Manufacturers of America. More people are even buying takeout for Thanksgiving, and a recent GMA survey found that almost half of shoppers won't buy *anything* that requires more than minimal preparation. Martha Stewart's new magazine, *Everyday Food*, lists just four ingredients for mustard-glazed salmon and even (gasp) suggests such shortcuts as using canned beans, frozen corn, and store-bought ravioli.

Because many of today's "cooks" don't know how to do more than soft boil an egg, Kraft has simplified the recipes on its packages. It scrapped the word *truss* for "close the opening of the bird," and "coat with" has taken the place of *dredge*. A century ago, every household could kill a chicken for Sunday dinner. "A hundred years from now, will anyone even know how to make spaghetti and meatballs?" wonders Balzer.

Perhaps even spaghetti and meatballs will come in one box, à la Betty Crocker Complete Meals, guided by the cake-mix-theory: Open the box, stir the ingredients together, and feel as if you've baked. Convenience products such as washed spinach in microwavable bags, refrigerated shredded potatoes, ready-made salads, precubed cheese, precarved chicken breasts, and jarred bruschetta no longer stigmatize buyers who grew up on chicken nuggets and Wolfgang Puck frozen pizza, says Balzer.

The Incredible Shrinking Candy Bar

Candy companies, fearing that customers will balk at a price increase, have long downsized their bars instead. Then yogurt makers caught on. Dannon started the "weight-out," trimming its container from 8 to 6 ounces while holding the price steady. Colombo fired back with a TV spot mocking Dannon's diminuzation and promising to stay at 8 ounces.

Although we're increasingly eating on the run—and on the road (20 percent of all meals are eaten in the car), we *want* to eat at home, says Balzer—just with someone else doing the cooking. This has fueled the "meal replacement" business, starting with Chinese takeout food, supermarket roaster chickens, and pizza delivery and followed by Boston Market (née Boston Chicken), Borden's Classico Italian corner, Tyson Gourmet selections, DiGiorno Rising Crust pizzas, Oscar Mayer meals, and Taco Bell supermarket dinners, to name a few—and has transformed grocers into gourmet caterers.

Restaurants and fast-food chains have changed their menus to woo women. Taco Bell's Grande Meals are designed to drive in the minivan set, Burger King's "lighter" chicken sandwiches with just 4 grams of fat were engineered with women's waists in mind, and McDonald's introduced new McCafés, a separate area in its restaurants where customers can order coffees topped with cream decorated with cinnamon golden arches.

Salads have become a weapon in the burger wars. Wendy's initiated salad bars in 1979 but revved them up in 2002 with its Garden

Sensation line. Ads for McDonald's focus on their high-quality greens topped with hot chicken and Newman's Own salad dressing. (McDonald's also added fresh fruit to Happy Meals.) And Jack-in-the Box ads show surprised patrons discovering Jack's Ultimate Salads.

To sell the steak, restaurateurs traditionally have shown the sizzle—splashing, broiling morsels—or touted the price/value proposition. Trying to net women, Red Lobster served up emotion. For 3 years it showed people joyously splashing and romping in the waves to remind them of their passion for the sea—and hunger for fresh fish. Now it is asking customers to "Share the Love" to emotionally connect with each other and with seafood. "Extensive research shows [that] consumers view eating shellfish as a uniquely tactile, even sensual experience that's also social," says Red Lobster President Edna K. Morris. "Seafood (especially shellfish) has the power to bring people together like no other food."

Many chains have added interactive nutrition calculators to their Web sites and posted dietary information such as fat content on menu boards and brochures long before the 2006 federal government deadline for listing the amount of artery-clogging trans-fat. "The specter of the McDonald's lawsuit spooked chains that the restaurant industry could become the next tobacco," said Bob Goldin, executive vice president of Technomic, a restaurant consultancy. Don't stake money on getting an accurate read, though. The National Restaurant Association says that 70 percent of customers customize food choices when they order. A sandwich with 10 items or toppings can come in 3,628,800 varieties.

Yet, despite our concerns, we are eating rapaciously, relishing TV cooking shows, inhaling cookbooks, and ordering professional induction-heat cook tops and restaurant-style refrigerators. Subway's Jared was the rare fast-food campaign with a health message, says Neil Stern, partner at consultant McMillan Dolittle. "Yet few customers actually order its low-fat sandwiches." People like the concept but are more self-indulgent than sacrificial, said GMA Vice President Gene Grabowski. "Picture a young woman who eats fat-free pretzels for a midafternoon snack, salad and mineral water for dinner, and tops it off with a bowl of gooey chocolate ice cream. Her behavior represents a lot of people."

Consider what this means overall. Even as more people go vegetarian, high-end steak houses are among the fastest growing type of restaurant.

Light beer continues to sell well, but high-cal microbrews sell better. Double-stuffed Oreos outstrip the reduced-fat cookie. And at Hardee's, the fastest growing item is the Monster Burger: three 1/4-pound patties, three slices of cheese, six slices of bacon, mayonnaise, 900+ calories, and more than 70 grams of fat.

It's a time of "sin and salvation eating," says Strategic Resource Group manager Burt Flickinger III. People pong between extremes, yearning for food that is better than good—and good for them. Industry wonks call it "indulgification," meaning that companies are furiously cooking up products that are less, well, deleterious and more "crave-able." Food technologists, who in the last decade have devised orange bell peppers, golden raspberries, broccolini, and seedless, sweeter, watermelons the size of cantaloupes, are focused on getting the flavor of fats and cream into their foodstuffs without actually using fat or dairy. LifeSavers' Crème Savers, Minute Maid frozen dessert in Fruit & Crème Swirl, and Nabisco Newtons Snackable Dessert, for example, have undergone liposuction but are hardly austere. Hershey promoted sugar-free versions of its Reese's Peanut Butter Cups as "your recommended daily allowance of indulgence."

Kellogg euthanized Special K Plus. People liked its benefits but nixed its flavor. With Special K Red Berries the company took a different tack, proclaiming, "Looking good never tasted so great." In one TV spot, a husband won't count his wife's eating this as genuine "sacrificing." In another, an average woman awaiting a bus for work muses in a stream-of-consciousness monologue about sticking a size 6 label on a size 12 dress, missing an earlier bus, giving up doughnuts—maybe not—the buns and calves on a passing bike messenger, getting them herself on her "treadmill . . . somewhere." A title card urges her to go easier on herself. An announcer suggests how: "Sweet strawberries, crunchy flakes, just 110 calories. Special K Red Berries. Help yourself!"

Good Humor slashed the calories from various ice cream novelties, Kellogg's leeched 40 percent of the fat from Morningstar Farms' Better 'n Burgers, and TCBY (The Country's Best Yogurt) urged eaters to dig in. In one commercial, text over the flat tummy of a svelte, bikini-clad woman reads, "51 percent of Americans are overweight. . . . We have a solution. Eat more dessert."

Alas, so many have shown so little restraint that 51 million Americans are dieting (66 percent of them women), according to Simmons Market Research Bureau. But today's battle of the bulge is more about balance and pleasure than about quick fixes and deprivation, says Rachel Levin, senior project director at NPD Group. Stouffer's Lean Cuisine exudes this in a "Do something good for yourself" TV spot. Four women out for a power walk discuss what they ate for dinner last night. One had microwave popcorn and cold spaghetti. Another had a pint of ice cream. A third ate leftover pizza. The fourth, who feasted on "herb-roasted chicken in a rich creamy mushroom sauce with roasted red-skin potatoes, broccoli, and red peppers," evokes the others' ire and envy. The point is that you don't have to give up taste for nutrition, says Roz O'Hearn, director of brand affairs for Nestlé Prepared Foods Division.

In fact, flavors are getting more robust, perhaps a result of baby boomers' dulling taste buds, says the Institute of Food Technologists. Chinese, Italian, and Mexican/Tex-Mex are closing in on "plain American" fare. Our zeal for exotic flavors, hot spices, and twists is growing. Hellman's has a new bacon and tomato–flavored mayo; Heinz and Hershey have a new green ketchup and chocolate syrup, respectively; and chains such as Chipotle are expanding with upscale Mexican cuisine. It seems that the only feeding style not in demand is intravenous.

Also big are foods that prevent or treat a condition—"foodaceuticals" or "nutraceuticals." In this age of therapeutic food, menopausal women have made soy ubiquitous. (There's soy turkey, soy milk, soy yogurt, soy burgers, soy *everything*.) "Functional" beverages such as

Slim-Fast have gained weight helping others keep pounds off. And with the demographic shift from truck drivers and hunters to women on high-protein diets, jerky meat snacks tout nutrition more than shelf life. Berries have popped up everywhere: in cereals and in water, in smoothies and toastables, in nutrition bars, and even in booze. So have grab-and-go energy-enhancing bars.

In 2003, the milk producers turned from overall deprivation ("Awful things happen when you run out of milk") to a more women-specific approach. In one "Strength from Within" spot, X-rays of connected bones remind us that calcium wards off osteoporosis. In another, everything is locked in reverse. Workers, messengers, and traffic all stream backward in rush hour. One strong woman is able to plunge forward. Dannon's Actimel dairy drink is supposed to strengthen the immune system, and Stonyfield Farm yogurt's dietary fiber ingredient, inulin, is supposed to help absorb calcium. PepsiCo's Aquafina Essentials is a fruit-flavored bottled water laced with minerals and vitamins; its Quaker Nutrition for Women cereals contain calcium, soy, and folic acid. Nestlé and Colgate teamed up to develop "functional confectionary" gum and candies that whiten teeth and fight plaque.

Sometimes what needs placating is our fear of unsafe foods. Because of this concern, the "natural foods" industry should grow from $12 billion to $50 billion in the next 5 years, says PaineWebber analyst Mark Hanratty. Farmers' markets are popular partly because their produce is fresh and comes from a local source.

Sometimes the "condition" that needs healing is simply life stress. In "Sticking," a hassled office worker walks through her department one afternoon bombarded by aggravating phone calls, faxes, and the boss—all literally stuck to her. To lighten her load, she takes a midday Frappuccino break. (Starbucks has a vitamin-fortified version called Power Frappuccino to replace a meal.) Even Swanson is pitching its "TV dinner," invented in 1953 as emergency fare for busy housewives, as the contemporary ultimate comfort food. A beautiful taffeta-gowned woman scarfs down the dinner in her magnificent mansion and then licks the plate. "Fortunately, TV dinner etiquette still applies," a voice jests.

Rover and Fluffy

As a society, we are doggone nuts over our animal companions. We "own"—or are owned by—66 million cats, 58 million dogs, 88 million fish, 40 million birds, 13 million small animals (including rabbits, hamsters, and gerbils), and 8 million reptiles. Feeding them is largely women's work.

Fifty years ago, before commercial pet food existed, cats ate leftovers, butcher's scraps, and the occasional mouse that scampered by. Then marketing took off in the 1970s, and today the pet food shelf is the largest piece of real estate in the supermarket—bigger than juice, pasta, or even baby food.

After research showed that women (the alphas in most pets' worlds) resented having to dig the glop out of the can with a spoon, companies began to change the smell and consistency of pet food to make it more palatable for the human "princess." They also changed the marketing once they learned that women see dogs as dumb and perpetually immature and cats as grown children and something of an alter ego. They assigned human characteristics of language, thought, feelings, and needs to dogs and described women's relationship with cats as special, tender, and even sexy. Anthropomorphic ads largely treat dogs as the family baby and theatrically portray tabby as king and hero. Women spark to their self-sufficiency and low maintenance.

All this psychology is paying off for marketers as we ply Chloe with special foods as a testament of our love. The economy may be on the ropes, but the premium food biz is booming. More than three out of four pet owners buy premium pet foods, and 52 percent admit that they go out of their way to prepare special meals for their animals. Ninety-seven percent regularly buy doggie or kitty treats or prime cuts.

Whether preparing food for our pets, families, or company, women have changed not just what we eat but how we eat it. The recipe ingredient that hasn't changed, however, is taste. Make it convenient, make it nutritional, make it slimming, but most of all make it delicious.

11

Technology: Chips Aren't Just for Baking

Men quivered with desire before the blow-your-head-off intensity of Cambridge SoundWorks' hi-fi stereo speakers. Few of them lugged this cache to the cashier, however. SoundWorks delved into the matter, only to discover that women were vetoing the purchase. And many of the guys who managed to get the speakers home met resistance setting up their systems or showing them off.

Women didn't want those big, ugly black boxes in their living rooms. They'd conceal them behind plants, vases, and chairs, says Ellen Di Resta, principal at Design Continuum, the research firm SoundWorks hired to unravel the mystery of sales lagging enthusiasm. Its solution: Make the SoundWorks system look so cool that there would be no need to hide it. Thus the Newton series of speakers and home theater systems was introduced in 2001 in various colors and finishes and became the best-selling line in SoundWorks' history.

Consumer electronics stores are still male magnets, the soul of the macho machine. But there's an even greater force in this field. More often than not, before boys can take home their toys, they need spousal approval. In *Time*, Josh Quittner described the scene of guys assessing racks of receivers "heads cocked in concentration like prairie dogs before an approaching storm," while their women, "looking as if their teeth were being drilled," stood behind them. Everyone knew whose teeth would need to bite before that receiver could be received.

It's not just women's role as cop guarding the family coffers that is nudging consumer electronics in the unisex direction. Jewels and flowers no longer carry Mother's Day. A Consumer Electronics Association survey found that almost two of three women (64 percent) would rather receive a digital camera than half-carat stud earrings, and 58 percent would rather unwrap a high-definition TV set than a one-carat sparkler. When it comes to electronics, men are presumed to be the 800-pound gorilla, but women shell out $55 billion a year on them (49 percent of the total spent), and influence three of every four electronics purchases, says Sean Wargo, director of industry analysis for CEA. In recent years, Amazon.com has experienced such a spike in tech sales around Mother's Day that it now features gizmos front and center on its home page during May.

Women are more likely than men to buy a 25-inch TV, a portable boom box, and any "gizmo or gadget that keeps them connected," says CEA Vice President Karen Chupka. Nearly two of three women now own a cell phone; 2 years earlier, 49 percent did. Twenty percent own a laptop, up from 12 percent in 2000. And two of three times it is mom who buys the computer for the kids, according to IntelliQuest.

At the 2003 consumer electronics show, banners proclaimed, "Technology Is a Girl's Best Friend." A whole product showcase was devoted specifically to female-friendly products, and there was a series of conferences and events on understanding and promoting women's increased role in this world. Just a few years ago almost 80 percent of consumer electronics show attendees were men, said Chupka. At the 2003 show, just 60 percent were.

Flat-panel TVs are another "bug light" to women because of their "style" and "I can take it with me" size. Women call the carry handle on some models "empowering," says Bill Johannesen, director of sales strategy at Sharp Electronics. "Today there are more products that women feel are necessary or at least of higher priority than before. And with more of them in the workforce, they also seek the luxury of small rewards, just like men. It goes with their sense of empowerment and affluence."

Marketers play to these senses, as well as to the aesthetic one. Although purchase warranties, manufacturer's support, and service reputation are critical to complete a purchase, IntelliQuest found that an emotional presell gets the ball rolling.

Rather than wattage, Sony and Philips highlight the power of confidence its products inspire. In a spot set to "What a Day for a Daydream," a beautiful grandma plunges into shark-infested waters to cavort among the killers. Watching the tape later, her granddaughter wonders where grandpa was. "On the boat," her mom snorts somewhat derisively. An ad for Philips' home cinema collection features a young woman with the headline, "None of My Friends Go to the Movies Anymore. They Come Over to My Place Instead."

Panasonic concluded that while men are more concerned with brand and what the thing does, for women, style is a key consideration. Perhaps this is why a chic businesswoman carries a notebook like a high-tech handbag in a Samsung spot and Intel's Bunny People strut down a runway lofting oversize Pentium II chips. Words such as *subwoofer*, on the other hand, jar women's ears. "I want as little information as possible to make an intelligent purchase," snips Kim France, editor-in-chief of shopping magazine *Lucky*. "Many women just want permission to buy the cute version of something."

Some of this minimalist mind-set carries over to computers and software, which most women regard as time-saving tools, like a washer or dryer, to simplify their lives, not as toys to distract them from it. Emphasizing power bits and bytes won't get women to "click here," warns Bernadette Tracy, president of NetSmart America, which conducts surveys for Web marketers. What will, she says, is showing them how a service is fast, secure, and convenient or presenting a high-tech product as high-touch, suggesting how it will enhance their life.

More marketers are doing this as cyberspace becomes more of a chick hangout. In 2001, women surpassed men online and continue to dominate. So dependent are they on their technology that they would rather give up their microwaves than the Internet. Seven of 10 cannot imagine life without Web access, says Women.com.

This explains the about-face of Microsoft Chief Executive Officer Steve Ballmer, who once blew out his vocal cords trying to pump up his salesforce. No longer content to "put a PC in every home and on every desk," this man's man now aims to help people "realize their potential" through software, admittedly because he came to recognize the clout of soccer moms. The company's "Wouldn't it be cool if your computer could?" campaign struck a chord with women for seeming to celebrate them.

Despite their proven loyalty to their tech tutors, more than 40 percent of women feel uncomfortable shopping for electronics or suspicious that they have been taken, says Sharp's Johannesen.

They complain that in a consumer electronics store they are often ignored, condescended to, or overwhelmed with tech talk— very different from the guy who ambles over to the cosmetics counter and the beauty guide quickly engages him, asks a few simple questions, and makes a sale. Addressing women's unease here, Best Buy positioned greeters at the door to welcome women. And Circuit City revamped, to "emphasize a product's benefits, not its features," says Anne-Marie Austin Stephens, a Circuit City senior vice president. "Women care about how a product will improve their lives more than how something works."

What do women want in computers? Just what they want in cars: reliability, ease of use, and a reasonable price, in that order, says Cherie Piebes, IBM manager of marketing communications. When IBM introduced the personal computer, it identified what was then a new breed of buyer: ordinary folks who just wanted to open the box and start typing. Early ads used a Charlie Chaplin–like "Little Tramp" character from *Modern Times* to make its technology less daunting, the public less anxious, and itself less "big and bad." More recently Dell moved beyond its core techie audience to include engineering naifs by being so approachable.

Of course, it is a generalization, but the genders do use the Web differently. Men tend to wander in cyberspace, looking for amusement. "Women want a more efficient experience. They go online for specific information or to make a specific purchase, get it, and get off," says Jupiter analyst Anya Sacharow. Because women value human relationships so much, marketers try to create connections and bonds with them rather than "episodic consumer collisions." Many spawn online communities of commerce-defined needs ("metamarkets") around major life events—such as menopause, mothers of the bride, and mothers-to-be.

Women typically manage these events (hence Palm's $99 hand-held personal digital assistant Zire to help "family planners") and the making and warehousing of memories. Industry statistics suggest that women are 60 percent of primary users of all cameras and camcorders. They are more interested in convenience and ease of use than in white balance, scene modes, or red-eye reduction. "For women, photography is all about memories, not technology," says Judy Strauss-Sansone, vice president of photo and consumables for CVS Corporation.

A century ago, Eastman Kodak created the simple-to-use Brownie ("You push the button; we do the rest") to democratize photography. More recently, its Easy Share has become the top-selling digital camera by tackling women's intimidation. Polaroid reclaimed its precarious perch by demonstrating that its instant cameras have the unique ability to do more than merely record a moment; they *make* a moment. Other digital camera manufacturers have added automatic settings to simplify the process. Some makers of palm-sized point-and-shoot cameras are even pushing the notion of wearing them as a necklace.

Teaching Tidbit

Not long ago, Carnegie Mellon University (CMU) tallied its female students against the number of male students named Dave. Not so surprisingly, the Daves won. In the average undergraduate computer science department, just 1 of every 10 students is female. However, the CMU department acted to adjust its Dave-to-girl ratio by changing its policy to deemphasize prior experience in computer programming and emphasize other experience. By late 2000, 40 percent of the undergrads at the School of Computer Science were women.

In a typical year, according to ACNielsen, Americans buy 653 million rolls of film, 442 million blank audio- and videocassettes, 261 million recordable CDs, and 2.8 trillion batteries. In 1986, Eveready blew a fuse with its outrageous spiky-haired bad-boy Jacko snarling and smashing things to promote Energizer's new, longer-lasting alkaline battery. Women, who buy at least 60 percent of the batteries, turned a deaf ear to the maniac's ranting. Energizer quickly retreated and came up with a pink bunny to represent perseverance and long life and to appeal to women. (Duracell attempted to neutralize the Energizer bunny with its nasty battery-powered Putterman clan. Victims of second-rate batteries keel over to the Puttermans' raucous laughter. They were quickly defanged. Women found the weird semi-robotic family too mean-spirited.)

Few action, adventure, and combat computer and video games directly target women, but since Lara Croft debuted as a female Indiana Jones in 1996 (and subsequently leapt from video console to Hollywood film), some computer companies have begun to target this audience. Chrysler and Jeep have designed games for women. In 2003, 21 percent of players were female, according to San Francisco investment firm Jeffries and Company. The market's fastest growing segment? Women playing at work, says Forrester Research principal analyst Charlene Li.

Most digital women are passive targets of violence, but some new games feature strong, attractive female protagonists—as in the films *X2: X-Men United, The Matrix Reloaded,* and *Charlie's Angels: Full Throttle.* In one, the *Tomb Raider* star (now with a more realistically proportioned bosom) fights "womano a womano" with evildoers.

"Most female game characters are portrayed to be what men would like to have in women," said Nour Polloni, lead producer of

Atari's Kya: Dark Lineage. She rejected her male team's plan to put the tomboyish teen star Kya in a string bikini, opting to show less digital skin and more of her personality. "With Kya, we wanted not a fantasy girl, but for her to be charming, a bit sexy, but not overwhelmingly so."

In Microsoft's Tao Feng: Fist of the Lotus, a mammoth tattooed hulk slams a woman half his weight through a window. In games such as Cy Girls, Brute Force, WarCraft III: Reign of Chaos, and Enter the Matrix, female gladiators have just as much chance of winning as the males do, suggesting a new equality.

Fighting femmes don't just attract female players. They galvanize guys who want to see their faces more, says Liz Buckley, product manager for Majesco, which makes BloodRayne. Instead of showing their vicious seductive vampire woman only from the rear while she tackles challenges, which is the norm in action-adventure games, players can see her face and pointy teeth, her blood-red hair, and her décolletage.

Reach Out and Touch Someone

Ronald Reagan was known as the great communicator.
He was the wrong sex.

ANONYMOUS

Back in the predawn of technology in 1981, AT&T won America's heart and dialing digit with "Joey Called," a commercial in which an aging middle-class black woman sobs because her grown son has phoned for no reason other than to say he loves her.

AT&T knew then what Bell Atlantic, Omnipoint, Sprint, MCI, Verizon, Worldcom, and every other purveyor of chat has since learned: Women like to talk. Tugging at their hearts is one way to give them permission to go at it.

Men make slightly more use of cell phones, but women make a whole lot more residential long-distance calls, says Tom Messner, a principal at Euro RSCG. Soon after "Joey" rang in, Messner engineered a parody on behalf of feisty MCI. This time mom weeps when she sees her humongous phone bill. (Interestingly, the mother-to-children phone connection is second in popularity to the sister-to-sister tie, he says.)

Either way, when it comes to phone plans, women pick more of them than men do. They own as many mobile phones, beepers, and personal digital assistants as their complementary gender and are in most pairings the social secretaries. They are the ones buying the greeting cards and baby shower and housewarming gifts, and they are the ones dispatching the thank-you notes.

They are also the ones to reach. When Deutsche Telekom bought VoiceStream wireless in 2001, it renamed the company T-Mobile and replaced Jamie Lee Curtis as spokeswoman with the more international Catherine Zeta-Jones. Its own research supported using a female endorser. "Women are just more accepting of women endorsers. And men look for a logical connection in male spokespeople but are okay with women not having a direct link to a product," says John Clelland, senior vice president of marketing at T-Mobile. In ads, Zeta-Jones freezes real-life vignettes to point out how a T-Mobile device could come in handy. In one spot she urges two women who find a ceramic toad for $1 at a tag sale to use their T-Mobile camera phone to e-mail a photo to an antiques dealer. He appraises the piece at $1 million.

At first, Cingular Wireless dialed a purely emotional play. Renowned artist and cerebral palsy sufferer Dan Keplinger struggles to paint fiery red streaks via a stick attached to his head and declares himself, with distorted words translated in subtitles, to be "unbelievably lucky." Then, "What do you have to say?" prodded the tagline. However, plucking the tear ducts wasn't enough in a category where features matter. Cingular switched to a harder sell at the same time, showing how its service improves peoples' lives. A dad uses Cingular's 7-to-7 plan, in which nighttime minutes start 2 hours earlier than other services, to talk with his son en route home from work, and young-adult triplets use the Family Talk plan to stay connected.

Verizon helped a young couple reconnect after a lover's spat tore them apart. "Scott" tries to make up with "Catherine" by leaving 17 voicemails, faxing an apology, and e-mailing photos of himself singing, "All I Need Is You." Finally, she relents when he shows up at her door in the pouring rain.

AT&T land lines' "Talk is good" campaign emotionally focuses on the "big issues" in our world and communities. While David Crosby sweetly sings "Thank You for Hearing Me," each issue—cloning, war, and prayer in schools—is presented on a title card followed by a question mark, as if to prompt a discussion. "Opinions may separate us. Miles don't have to," says the narrator, explaining that AT&T's local calling area is larger than that of other carriers.

For AT&T Wireless, the emotional hot button was freedom. Ads suggested that its mLife is *the* mobile way to live unfettered, cutting the umbilical cord in a birth scene as a metaphor of emancipation.

Gender Calls

When it comes to phones, men and women prefer different fiberoptics. A PrimeCo Personal Communications survey shows that men are 66 percent more likely to use their wireless phones in the bathroom, whereas women are equally more likely to snoop through their partners' phone bill looking for suspicious numbers. Their fingers do the walking differently, too. "Auto parts, new and used" is the category men consult most often in the Yellow Pages, whereas for women it's "Physicians and surgeons," according to the Yellow Pages Publishers Association.

Check the handwriting. Chances are that the anniversary or birthday card from dad, your brother, or even your husband wasn't actually signed by him. Most women buy and write the cards to their husband's family. Men find the cardboard printed with corny greetings and adolescent toilet jokes useless, says Michael Peck, writing in the *Washington Post.* "They do not tell you how to fix cars or pick a winning stock. Better to use a cell phone to leave a greeting while you are stuck in traffic (and have their spouses make social calls, otherwise known as 'male telephobia')."

More than guys suffering from "cardophobia," it's that women have "cardophilia." The Greeting Card Association says that women buy at least 80 percent of its merchandise: Hallmark says 90 percent. For women, Hallmark Moments are an opportunity to bond, and those soft, gauzy images of playful kittens or mischievous pooches attached to a message are the architecture of a support network.

Name a milestone or occasion, and women want to celebrate or commemorate it. Because so many regularly send notes in their pets' names, greeting card companies now target the pet lover in them. "To a Mother Everyone's Mutts About," reads one of three canine cards Hallmark offered for Mother's Day 2003. Two other varieties pretend to come from cats. American Greetings' Carlton line had five animal companion cards, and recycled Paper Greetings ranks pet cards among its best-sellers.

Greeting cards "reflect the day, the culture, and the time," says Hallmark spokeswoman Rachel Bolton. "A few decades ago, we wouldn't have made it [referring to pet greetings], and you wouldn't have bought it." In the 1980s, cards were more sentimental. People opted for messages that evoked the way they hoped things would be. Nowadays they are as likely to go for irreverence or gentle humor as for a straight message.

Warm, uplifting, sweet, and "keepsake-able" is what sells but nothing where the message is too cutesy, says Pat Barker, senior vice president of Hallmark's creative product development. A card with a photo of two hermit crabs that reads, "Thanks for loving me even when I'm crabby" is a best-seller. Although mean or sarcastic humor works, this house of cards disdains it. It's not Hallmark's way to poke fun at people's jobs or physique.

It is Hallmark's way to research what works for which audience. Dads, for example, feel good when you list all they do, but moms resent it "because it seems like you're listing all the things she had to do," says Mark Mills, editorial director for Hallmark's "Masculine Relative Birthday." Dads also respond well to "I seldom say," whereas brothers appreciate the "you were a little pest but now a great friend" theme. "People often say [that] Hallmark must be spying on me, or how could they know exactly how I was feeling?" adds Barker.

Old world primness and propriety may be a dwindling remnant from the days of Jane Eyre, but the one communication arena where women still need some coaxing is posting personals. Yahoo understood this and sought a distinctive positioning compared with "category killer" Match.com. Soft, humble spots (versus Match.com's loud and proud ones) explore the anxious, excited, hopeful terrain of first dates. While soldiers in the search of love prepare for battle—brushing, shaving, plucking, and smoothing—we share their reveries and aspirations. The ad ends with a yodel and one word—*Believe*—while an animated flower erupts.

Electronic products and the programs to sell them have changed as women have ventured into the heretofore male magnet stores, not just as a cop conferring "spousal approval" but as the real 800-pound gorilla shopper.

12

Homes and Homebase

A man's home may be his castle, but a woman's is her kingdom. From blenders to balustrades, cookware to curtains, wingbacks to wainscoting, women are overwhelmingly the ones responsible for making a house a home. They buy 90 percent of the furnishings and select 89 percent of the homes. They initiate four of five home-improvement projects, according to Women's Entertainment LLC, and increasingly, they are the ones wielding the hammer.

"There's still a 'damsel in distress/knight in shining armor' mentality when it comes to women and home repair," concedes Allegra Bennett, author of *When a Woman Takes an Ax to a Wall.* But there are fewer helpless hausfraus standing by clueless while their mates tackle the leaky faucet. More and more women are "experiencing that sense of empowerment that comes with fixing something they were afraid of," Bennett says.

In 2001, Ms. Fix-It bought 40 percent of repair/renovation equipment, according to the Home Improvement Research Institute in Tampa. Consequently, companies have begun designing tools with smaller grips that are "friendlier, more ergonomic, and lighter weight," said Craftsman Tools spokesman Bob Vila.

When her young son was locked in the bathroom and she didn't have the necessary Allen wrench or hex key to jimmy the lock, Barbara Kavovit was abashed at her own helplessness. So she founded (and is now CEO of) Manhattan-based Anchor Construction, which turns out lightweight turquoise claw hammers and slip-joint pliers with sculptured rubber handles. And Tomboy Tools sells its woman-friendly home-repair equipment at "tool parties" at women's homes. Its Web-site slogan: "No pink tools!"

Sherwin Williams changed its colors for women. The paint retailer expanded its palette to 1400 shades, moved its ads off ESPN to women-centric programs, showed a woman bringing in a china teapot to match a paint sample, and invented a female-friendly, easy-open twist-top plastic container to banish the round metal can women loathed. The Dutch Boy paint "can" has a built-in side handle and a no-drip spout that guides the gunk back inside because "women care about ease of use and being neat," said Adam Chafe, director of marketing for Dutch Boy. Thus there is no splattering paint (which inevitably happens when you pry off and tamp back on that clunky metal lid), no need for super finger strength to hoist the old pail-type handle, and no messy drips.

Women also have invaded the heretofore male inner sanctum of the hardware store. Half the customers at Lowe's are female, up from 13 percent in the late 1980s. The chain widened aisles, brightened lighting, installed child seats on its heavy-duty shopping carts, and altered its former lumber shop ambiance to appeal to females, says Dale Pond, executive vice president for merchandising. Ace Hardware changed its "helpful hardware man" motto to "the helpful hardware folks," and Sears, which has watched the number of its female Crafts-man Club members soar, has shown the repair "man" as a woman.

Home Depot has added decorating services, boosted its appliance offerings, and expanded its do it-yourself clinics for women, teaching them everything from how to fix the storm drain to how to rewire the den. Its 2003 "You can do it: We can help" ads (which debuted during the women-watched Grammy Awards), preach empowerment. In one, a single woman retiles her hallway beautifully, dispelling her dad's doubts. In another, a happy mom warns her college-student son that his former bedroom is now a luxury bathroom. The ads go beyond Home Depot's fundamental premise of great price, assortment, and service to "take a more personal look at our shoppers who are focused on making their homes a sanctuary," says John Costello, chief marketing officer. A Home Depot survey found that 37 percent of women would rather do a home-improvement project than shop and that 54 percent of its female customers versus 51 percent of men are currently involved in a task.

Home Statistics

According to the Home Improvement Research Institute:
- Eighty percent of all female homeowners do minor repairs themselves.
- A third tackle larger home-beautification projects.
- Ten percent are serious do-it-yourselfers, comfortable with contractor-worthy tasks such as building decks and removing a wall.

In hardware retailer Canadian Tire's 2003 catalog there's nary a picture of a cordless power drill, gas barbecue, Stillson wrench, or Michelin tire. Instead, there are pastel images of place settings and soft-focus shots of tea towels and kitchen gadgets. "Spring . . . bring it on," the text gushes. "We're ready to clean out the cobwebs, open the windows, crisp up the curtains, and let the light shine into every corner of the house." Spokeswoman Lisa Gibson says Canadian Tire has long been regarded as a guy store, but really, its customer base is half female, and concentrating on women won't alienate "those who don't know a garlic press from a bench press." Men won't give the blenders and ice-cream makers a second glance en route to the lumber or whatever it is they're interested in, she says.

Black & Decker hosts power tool seminars for women to try out hand drills, sanders, and saws and overcome power tool intimidation. It also ran a quirky spot for its Navigator power saw that only at the end revealed that the tool had been wielded by a white-haired woman in a housedress and tool belt. (According to Black & Decker, the first item a woman usually buys is a cordless screwdriver. Then comes a drill, saw [circular or jigsaw], and sander.)

PBS show "Handy Ma'am" host Beverly DeJulio says that the 10 essential tools women should have include a set of screwdrivers (three sizes of slotted and three sizes of Phillips head screwdrivers), a 16-ounce awl claw hammer, a small and a medium-sized adjustable wrench, three pliers (slip joint, tongue-and-groove long-handled, and needle-nose), a utility knife, a retractable metal tape measure, an all-purpose saw, and safety goggles. And it's good, she says, to have an assortment of nails, screws, tape (electrical, masking, and duct), sandpaper, and a strong glue on hand.

Even the barbecue, manned by the Mr., probably was selected by the Mrs. Before Sunbeam designed, positioned, and launched a new line of Coleman gas barbecue grills, its research discovered that its principal customers didn't see a gas grill as a tool to cook hot dogs "so much as the centerpiece of warm family moments worthy of a summer highlights reel," says Danene Jaffe, senior director of strategic planning. Thus Coleman repressed the urge to talk of BTUs, rotisserie options, and cooking square inches. Instead, both the grill and marketing were designed to evoke nostalgia for the camping experience with friends and family as "a relaxing ritual where the grilling area is the stage," an event that takes place in a "backyard oasis." It made for one of the most successful launches in Sunbeam's history. On the other hand, men buy the vacuum cleaners, so they're sold by their amperage or raw power—because market research says male shoppers want "maximum suck."

Delta knows that women turn their kitchen faucets on and off more often than men (on average, 22 times a day versus 16 for men), but this is not why its ads speak to them. "They're the decision makers," says President John Wills. Seventy-five percent of Zircon hardware sales are to women. MasterLock abandoned the Super Bowl after 21 years when it concluded that women are in charge of lockup.

Orkin Pest Control runs funny ads. In one, a cockroach crawls across the screen looking so real that some viewers tried to kill it, and in another the company shows the extremes people go to—wind tunnels and igloo thermostats—to avoid the "ick factor." It recognizes that women make the decisions on everything from basic services to costlier termite protection, said Steve Danuser, vice president of marketing. And after Owens Corning discovered that women initiated 75 percent of service calls, it scrapped its traditional masculine guys in trucks wearing uniforms and toting big toolboxes to show a confident woman in the foreground with the repairman working in the rear. "The prime message was here's a man who comes when you call him," said Chuck Stein, vice president and general manager for Owens Corning HOMExperts. Focus groups reassured Owens Corning that women would identify with the ad and men wouldn't care. "For us, the hero was the empowered woman getting her home just the way she wants it," says Stein.

Getting her home just as she wants it is what Pier 1 Imports offers. Seven of every 10 of its customers are female, says Phil Schneider, senior vice president of marketing. Swedish retailer Ikea's ads aim to show how it's got the goods to make your place look good—and the experience of shopping for it is so comfortable that it feels like home. In "Kitchen," a wife "stuck in here like some prisoner" accuses her husband of "prowling the streets" when a salesman interrupts the ugly argument to ask what they think. They appraise their surroundings and declare, "It feels good; we'll take it." In "Living Room," a sullen teen tells her parents that she's pregnant, and her dad blames her "creepy boyfriend" and her mom for smoking dope in college. The Ikea rep butts in to inquire how they are. The family glances around the beautifully assembled showroom display and decides to take it.

Other playful ads encourage women to lighten up (literally) and bring home new stuff just for the fun of it. In one spot, as poignant music swells, a woman buys a new lamp and discards the old one in a driving rain. "Many of you feel bad for this lamp," says a man with a Swedish accent who materializes on the sodden street. "That is because you're crazy. It has no feelings, and the new one is much better." Pottery

Barn is also pushing the message that furniture is like fashion—changeable—and Corian wants people to think of its countertops like carpeting—to be replaced frequently.

Stanley Steemer is angling to get an occasional activity done more often. Ads show people pumping gas, plowing through construction zones, and racing up and down school-bus aisles—eventually hauling home all that dirt underfoot. The point: Professional carpet cleaning should be more than an annual ritual or a reaction to a major spill.

Serial renovators have buoyed sales throughout the house. They have made elaborate security systems, multidimensional lighting, and "uber appliances" such as Miele's $1900 built-in coffeemaker, Aga's $12,000 stove, and Maytag's $6000 Jade refrigerator in the kitchen common. When Maytag introduced its front-loading Neptune washer in 1997, critics expected the $1000 washer would be all dried up when the average price for other washers was $424. They were wrong.

But where the vacation-at-home mantra shows up most noticeably is the bathroom. More than half of today's new homes have at least 2.5 bathrooms, compared with just 25 percent in 1980. No longer plain-Jane 5- by 7-foot "Johns," bathrooms are living centers and the ultimate status symbol. Often they are so spacious and elegant that people use them as offices, dens, fitness centers, and places to unwind.

Plumbing fixtures have become a fashion statement, winning their first starring role in 1978 in the "Bold Look of Kohler" campaign. This presented everyday fixtures in attention-grabbing, surreal settings that appealed more to the women living in the house than the contractor altering it. In addition to double motion-sensor sinks and power-flush toilets, these new oases house coffeemakers, TVs, steam shower systems with jets and massage features, mood lighting, heated towel racks and floor tiles, and deep bathing-pool-like tubs. (Whirlpools are so yesterday.) Jacuzzi's two-person bath/entertainment center features surround sound, a flat-screen TV, a DVD player, a CD player, and a floating remote control. "Bathrooms are all about destressing—relaxing, refreshing, rejuvenating, retreating," said Jacqueline Marquardt, senior product manager at Kohler.

Women's toilet training has even changed the look (and odor) of public Porta-Potties. "Men will go behind a tree. We cater to women who leave parties when the restrooms aren't up to par," said Dave Bandauski, president of Black Tie Services, one of the many upscale mobile restroom operations whose amenities include tuxedoed attendants, brass fixtures and oak paneling, vanity mirrors, flushable toilets, full sinks, piped-in music, air conditioning, potpourri, fresh flowers on marble countertops, carpeted floors, and real towels. Women are even responsible for the toilet seat protection shields in the less accommodating public loos.

Women are also the impetus for most of the innovations in household cleaning products because they are the home's primary sanitation engineer—and none too happy about it. Oxo devised an ergonomic soap-dispensing scrub wand to dispatch burgundy wine stains, and Bissell's Steam Mop can banish muddy footprints from tumbled limestone fast. Evercare's Large Surface Lint Pick-Up, a giant version of lint rollers with tear-off sticky layers, tackles hair on the bathroom floor. A female team at Procter & Gamble came up with the Swiffer floor cleaner that doesn't "just move it" but removes it. To engage women in the cleaning process "rather than having [them] just push the beast around the floor," Hoover used a clear plastic cup in its SteamVac. "People like to see the dirty water coming out. They feel like they are accomplishing something," says Marketing Vice President Dave Baker.

For years, General Electric has turned women on to its light bulbs by reminding them, with warm, fuzzy images, how GE brings good things to life. Recently it came out with Reveal lightbulbs, which make things look richer, more vivid, and less yellow and can instantly make a room over for a fraction of the cost of redecorating, says Ken Damato, GE Lighting's general manager of consumer marketing.

Philips tried a different tack to light up this inherently indifferent, unemotional category. Recognizing that there is no good time for a lightbulb to blow, that changing it is a nuisance, and that making that happen less often is a marketing opportunity, its zany ads show the sometimes hilarious situations that happen when the lights go out. In one, a rotund matron laments that the magic has gone out of their marriage. "Every time the lights go out, you fall asleep," she tells her soup-slurping husband. Sure enough, the lights go out and from the darkened screen come snores and sputters.

Single Women on Their Own

Even while home ownership for couples has declined in the past 15 years, it has increased 25 percent for women living alone. Single women make up the second largest group of homebuyers after couples, according to the National Association of Realtors, with a homeownership rate of 57 percent. Single women buy homes at twice the rate of single men.

Whatever it is that makes a house a home, chances are it's women's doing. From kitchen appliances to bathroom plumbing to dining room wallpaper to den wingbacks, Ms. Fix-It is on the case. She's grown up from that little girl "playing house" to furnishing and running it today.

13

You Throw Like a Girl

Espn's audience is 75 percent male. Fans of both sexes prefer watching guys on the court. The Women's National Basketball Association (WNBA) has been closing franchises, and female soccer players earn less than they did a few years ago. At the same time, women are becoming the stars of sports marketing.

In the U.S. Tennis Open, it is the women (okay, the Williamses) who captivate the crowd with their personalities, skill, and flashes of glamour. On the greens it was Annika Sorenstam who galvanized a huge and enthusiastic gallery that cheered her long drives, groaned at her missed putts, and rode the emotional roller coaster at the Colonial Country Club in Fort Worth along with the first woman to play a PGA Tour event since Babe Didrikson Zaharias in 1945. Iron Mike had nothing on "celebrity boxers" Tonya Harding versus Paula Jones. And in July 1999 when soccer star Brandi Chastain dropped to her knees and triumphantly tore off her jersey after scoring the decisive penalty kick against China to win the Women's World Cup, it was a moment of ecstatic release, of celebration, and of confirmation.

"That was a crowning moment for women everywhere, a moment of freedom, of liberation," says Marlene Bjornsrud, general manager of the San Jose CyberRays, the team for which Chastain plays. It's a sharp contrast to the late 1970s when the judges insisted that for Jan Todd, professor of kinesiology at the University of Texas, to compete in power lifting, she had to play by the same rules as men, She would have to weigh in, in the buff, before a panel of male adjudicators, and during show time, she would have to wear a jockstrap and go braless. Dr. Todd opted to give "exhibitions" instead.

While the endorsement contracts of women athletes amount to a hill of beans compared with Michael Jordan's, the amount women spend on athletic equipment is well worth cultivating. Since Title IX (which forbade sex discrimination in educational programs receiving federal funds) was enacted in 1972, the number of girls kicking soccer balls and shooting baskets in high school soared from 1 in 27 to 1 in 3, the Women's Sports Foundation says. Women's participation in college sports has grown fivefold since then, the foundation adds, and the number of women who participate in "fitness activities" more than 100 times a year increased 24 percent from 1990 to 2000. In a recent year, 52 percent of the 58 million Americans who worked out at a health club were female, says the International Health, Racquet and Sports Club Association. Clubs such as Lucille Roberts, Curves for Women, Contours Express, and Slender Lady cater exclusively to them. (Alas, Title IX is under review because critics claim it discriminates against men, shuttering their programs to create new ones for women. In truth, what's squeezing athletic budgets is football, with its bloated squads and coaches' salaries.)

More than half of all women don cross-trainers, runners, or some other sport shoes daily, up from 42 percent in 1995. Women spend around $3 billion of the $15 billion shelled out annually on golfing gear and fees. And the engine rev lures both genders: Thirty-eight percent of NASCAR fans are women, as are 31 percent of fans who attend an auto race at least once a month, according to Mediamark Research, Inc. Forty percent of spectators at National Hockey League games are women. Women have made gymnastics, ice hockey, and figure skating among the most watched Olympic events.

Sporting goods makers now tailor products specifically for women. Rawlings Sporting Goods offers 12 models of women's softball gloves—designed for smaller hands. The Dot Richardson Louisville Slugger bat comes with a scaled-down grip, and batting helmets now come with ponytail holes in back. Bicycle seats have been reconfigured, golf bags and tennis rackets have been lightened, and inline skates have been narrowed. Nike heightened the arch and narrowed the heel cup on its women's basketball shoes. And after a year of testing, K2 introduced the T Nine Series of skis (named for Title IX) that are lighter and softer than most men's models.

Marketers on the fringes of the athletic world have recognized this female influx. At the height of sandal season, Lamisil Athlete's Foot Cream let women know that athlete's foot is an equal opportunity fungal infection. Corporate research showed that 26 percent of women have had it; most misdiagnosed it and treated the symptoms with moisturizers.

When women's athletic clothing company Athleta mailed its first catalog in 1998, the women's sportswear industry was somnolent. The giants, such as Nike, were focused on men. Now that women spend around $25 billion a year here—market research firm Packaged Facts expects it to balloon to $38 billion by 2005—everyone from Prada to Victoria's Secret has an athletic line. Nike even has stores called Nike Goddess.

Liz Claiborne developed a line of golf clothes. Callaway, Taylor Made, Goldwin, Top-Flite, Tommy Armour, Mizuno, and Yonex joined Cobra, Square Two, and Lange in making women's clubs. And in 2001, Precept's MC Lady was the second-best-selling golf ball: 98 percent of its purchasers were men. Initially, they sheepishly claimed they were buying the Lady for their wives. Then they took to calling it "the Laddie." Ultimately, they openly played with it, driving demand to unmeetable levels.

Because 43 percent of National Football League (NFL) fans are female, the league launched a women's clothing line in 1997. Ditto for the National Basketball Association (NBA). Jerseys from the major sports leagues (NBA, NFL, MLB, and NHL) that are refitted and restyled as dresses are sailing out of ballparks. Within 6 months of delivering its first sports-jersey dresses, NBA and NFL licensee Reebok says they were a best-seller in its women's wear, buoyed by hip-hop star Eve and chanteuse Mariah Carey flaunting a gown made from two Michael Jordan jerseys.

Just 46 percent of attendees at Major League Baseball (MLB) games are female, but baseball is wantonly wooing them because women have the final say on family leisure activities and merchandise purchases, the commissioner's office says. And women are "seriously unfamiliar with ballpark amenities and packages." There are now reduced-price tickets on Mother's Day and "Ladies' Nights" and a "women's corner" on the MLB Web site.

So many women watch the Super Bowl that Oxygen Media debuted its ad campaign there. Tropicana Senior Vice President Roger Berdusco said that the game "has transcended from being a sporting event to a real social event." This is its prime lure for women. "For men, sports is social currency," said Artie Bulgrin, chief of research at ESPN. "They need to know what happened last night to talk about it with their buddies." Women enjoy its social aspects—the family gathered around the set, a group outing to a game—but are much less likely to watch alone, he said. Evolutionary anthropologist Helen Fisher says both genders enjoy the exercise and challenge of sports. "But for men it's also basic display behavior for impressing and winning a mate."

Women now shell out almost $5 billion a year on sport shoes alone. Until recently, most companies, like those that make men's shoes, touted their technological gadgetry. Yet surveys showed that more women choose a sports shoe for its looks than for its construction merits.

L.A. Gear introduced women's aerobics shoes just as the exercise fad took off. In 1997, designer Jil Sander's gold logo of her name on ladies Puma running shoes made Pumas cool. Concurrently, Skechers marketed its flat, comfy shoes as stylish. Nike started a woman's division in 2000; among its offerings: a Visi Mazy sling-back in woven fabric and "lime chill" and "midnight navy" colors, a split-toe Air Rift, an Air Max Specter, a slip-on sneaker inspired by the spiraling metallic towers of the Bilbao, and a new Kyoto cross-trainer for yoga devotees. The motto on its Nike Goddess Web site is, "Look Good. Kick Ass." And while Adidas claims that its ClimaCool shoes can control the heat inside, women are at least as interested in the hot colors on their outsides.

Marketers are revising their advertising as well as their products to attract sporting women. Years ago, when Nike reminded viewers that "Life Is Short" so they should "Play Hard" and Reebok preached that "No Pain [equals] No Gain," in a low-testosterone, holistic way, New Balance urged runners to "achieve new balance." In ads, a woman thought about how she could balance a hectic, fast-paced life or celebrated "renewing her license to dream and discovering that strong is beautiful." One line trumped with "One less woman walking in someone else's footsteps."

In graphically simple and strong ads in 2003, Brooks Sports pictured a solitary runner with her favorite shoes and an insight into her feelings. "Running is never lonely because I really like the woman I run with," one woman muses. K2 advised women to trade in their old in-line skates for new soft boots if they pick fights with other skaters, refuse to pick up after themselves, or do anything else that suggests that their skates may be "laced with a little too much testosterone." The tag reads, "Don't let the same number of toes fool you; women's feet are different from men's."

Soon after her husband Neal died of a heart attack in 1970 and Gertrude Boyle took over their floundering company, Columbia Sportswear ads dutifully showcased the garments' technical features and sturdy fabric. Over time, they came to showcase the brassy, bossy, impossible-to-please "tough mother," Gert, who, mortgaged to the hairline, enlisted her then 21-year-son Tim to turn their sports rags into riches. In one audacious ad, Gert, as an unstoppable engine mowing down whatever is in her path, is in a biker crowd, glaring over her trademark bifocals while the camera caresses the "Born to Nag" tattoo on her arm. In another, Tim accidentally knocks Gert off a cliff and then hauls her back up with his strong-as-nails Columbia jacket.

Gert got to the girls, but nowadays it's female athletes getting the calls, says Scott Becher, president of Sports and Sponsorships. The WNBA attracted such tony sponsors as American Express, Bud Light, Champion, Coca-Cola, General Motors, Kellogg, Lee Jeans, McDonald's, and Sears, and Venus and Serena Williams have attracted corporate contracts from Reebok to Wrigley's gum, Avon to Wilson clothing, Nortel Networks to a Sega video game. "For the first time, advertisers are paying females at a value normally associated with male athletes," says Bob Williams, president of Burns Sports Celebrity Service, Inc. Mountain Dew has used chicks along with dudes in its extreme sports ads. And Sorenstam swings her Great Big Bertha II driver in Callaway ads as a headline notes, "Great shots mean you can play with the boys."

The "boys" will most likely resist. Guys finishing behind Sorenstam were mocked—*Sports Illustrated* columnist Rick Reilly suggested that tampons might be left in their lockers—because guys largely see losing to women as emasculating. The girl code, meanwhile, equates beating a boy at anything with doom, says child psychologist Sylvia Rimm, author of *See Jane Win*. "It meant no boy would ever want to have you as a girlfriend."

These "codes" are much less binding today than they were three decades ago, when Billie Jean King played a tennis match against Bobby Riggs. More and more women are competing against men. Julie Krone has won a Triple Crown race. Sarah Fisher competed in her fourth Indy 500 in 2003. Katie Hnida kicked in the Las Vegas Bowl. Shawna Robinson drove in stock car racing's Winston Cup. And while not exactly going head to head *with* men, Michelle Kwan won her seventh national women's figure skating championship after flawlessly executing the same jumps as most men and looking stronger and better doing it.

The ritual Brandi Chastain performed, of ripping off her jersey, is now prohibited for both men and women. But that muscular and euphoric image embedded in our mind's eye is closer to the reality of women in sports than figure skaters in their sparkly dresses or the injured gymnast Kerri Strug weeping as her coach carried her away after winning the gold at the 1996 games. Says Sue Levin, CEO of Lucy Active-wear: "It is the image of a self-actualized woman who just conquered the world."

14

When Sales Dip, Men's Products Discover Women

Liquor: Drink Up

Even as brewers and distillers continue to tease men with the prospect of getting under women's skirts, they've begun talking directly to "the skirts." While they still beam most of their ads at twenty-something men, more of them are talking to women, coming up with some softer-tasting products and pitches and watching their language and calorie counts. Light beer is the fastest growing type of beer and the one "the skirts" drink.

Light, citrus-flavored malt beverages, a.k.a. "malternatives," pick up where wine coolers of the 1980s left off. Coors pioneered here with Zima in 1993—it was immediately branded a "chick drink"— and then followed up with berry-flavored Vibe. Smirnoff Ice, Skyy Blue, Bacardi Silver, Stoli Citrona, and Captain Morgan Gold chimed in, promoting their candied beers as new and sexy. In ads, tanned women in white bathing suits smile and drink from dark blue bottles that look like Skyy vodka bottles. A female hand reaches in and steals away a sweating bottle of Bacardi Silver. The half-naked buff guy shaving in the steamy bathroom follows.

Fruit-flavored wines are also gaining traction. "Arbor Mist is to women what beer is for guys," declares Rob Vlosky, category director for the Canandaigua Wine Company. When the guys in a commercial ask for some Arbor Mist that the women are enjoying poolside, they resist ("This is our drink"), so the men perform tricks for it, including an exhibition of synchronized swimming. An ad for Seagram's cooler proclaiming, "It's what women like," showed a toilet with its seat in the down position.

Distillers admit that Scotch has a problem with women: Four of five of those who drink Scotch are male. Therefore, the whiskey makers have devised such cocktails as the Rob Roy (a froth of Scotch and vermouth) to lay claim to women's palates. This, as well as pink daiquiris and margaritas, worked for a while. But today's young women don't want their mother's drink. So, in addition to its spoofy Vegas-style lounge parties with Playboy bunnies to recall Scotch's heyday and throw men a bone, Dewar's asked the hip proprietor of a downtown Manhattan club, the Flatiron Lounge, to come up with a sequel to serve at tastings it sponsors for graduate students, half of whom are women. Julie Reiner concocted Vamp, a smoky blend of Scotch and fresh orange juice that's carbohydrate-free and lower in sugar than most "women drinks."

Since Brown-Forman Corporation introduced Southern Comfort more than a century ago, it has targeted young status-minded men. Recently, it also began picturing women showing other women how to use its bourbon in recipes and other drinks. And it introduced Southern Twist, a sweet, fruity derivation of Southern Comfort with you-know-who in mind.

You-know-who is also quaffing down just what men do. Five years ago women bought 40 percent of the wine sold in America. Today they are buying 60 percent. Michael Mondavi, chief executive officer of Robert Mondavi Wineries, expects that this will top 70 percent by 2005. Women also buy 55 percent of the champagne. Perhaps more surprising, they also take home over half the cognac and most other liquor generally assumed to put hair on one's chest.

Back in the late 1930s, only one of Alcoholics Anonymous' 100 founding members was female. Women led the temperance movement and for a while privately imbibed at home. Now many members of the "girl power" generation go shot for shot with the guys; they see holding their liquor as a feminist badge of honor. (Besides waking up in the emergency room, they are also getting arrested more, doing drugs more, and generally behaving more like guys in other rambunctious ways.) A sweet 16 today is four times more likely to have gotten into the booze as her mom did at that age. She's yielding to peer pressure for sure, but it's not so much to impress boys as to click with other girls. Devon Jersild, author of *Happy Hours: Alcohol in a Woman's Life*, says that women "associate drinking with power, and they think that if they drink like a guy, they will be like a guy."

More women than men attend alcohol abuse screenings at federally funded daylong clinics. And universities from Stanford to the University of Vermont to the University of Colorado at Boulder to Georgetown report surges in coed intoxication, regretful sex while drunk, and alcohol violations. A study by Henry Wechsler of the Harvard School of Public Health found that between 1993 and 2001, frequent binge drinking increased 125 percent at all-women colleges. Dr. Duncan Clark of the Pittsburgh Adolescent Alcohol Research Center expects alcohol abuse between men and women to ultimately level out in "a perverse kind of equality."

Liquor companies actually began chasing women in the mid-1970s, but that was a mere advertising trickle compared with today's deluge, when fashion magazines brim with beguiling beauties reveling in their candy-colored cocktails. "Get in touch with your masculine side," instructs one recent Jim Beam ad in which a woman puffs on a cigar. Naked women wrapped in orange peels hold Cointreau bottles while urged to "Be Cointreauversial."

Winemakers also have started telling the distaff sex that this Sauvignon's for them. Overall, Americans are seemingly wine intimidated and averse. Americans sip just a sixth of what Italians do and, at 2 gallons a year per person, trail 31 other nations, according to *International Wines and Spirits*. In contrast, the average American chugs 22 gallons of beer a year. "Wine is not a part of daily life here where beer and Coca-Cola are," Wine Market Council President John Gillespie says glumly.

This is about to change. Wineries are transitioning from "a cottage industry of gentleman farmers into a consumer-products, luxury-goods industry," says Michael Mondavi. Not long ago, winemakers spent less on ads than even on eyeglasses and corrective lenses and just slightly more than on room deodorizers. However, with multinational giants such as Diageo, Southcorp, Brown-Forman, and Constellation Brands snapping up small wineries, they are infusing marketing muscle and moxie into magnums.

Mondavi, which for years spent almost nothing advertising its Woodbridge brand, is now all over TV, along with E. J. Gallo and Beringer Blass Wine Estates. Clos du Val Wine Company struck deals to get its wine featured on *The Sopranos*. Instead of showing a bottle draped with awards or family members earnestly boasting about their winery's heritage in the occasional ad, new spots tout the joy, sociability, and emotional lift from wine in hopes of converting marginal or special-occasion drinkers into all-occasion wine-with-dinner people.

Winemakers are uncorking even more gusto than in the late 1970s, when huge consumer-product conglomerates such as Coca-Cola and RJR Nabisco owned jug wine divisions and sponsored Orson Welles' sober pronouncement to "sell no wine before its time." Their goal is to do to wine what "the other white meat" did for pork, says veteran industry consultant Jon Fredrikson.

Restaurants also have joined the crusade. Olive Garden hypes wine at its restaurants, training staff about it and plying waiting customers with free Gallo tastings. "Wine can be very intimidating," notes William Edwards, the chain's director of beverage strategy. "But let people taste it, and they understand [that] it doesn't have to be scary."

Even beer, the last bastion of "boy buying," is trying to get in touch with its feminine side. Women represent a 25 percent and growing share of the market, says Frank Walters, research director for industry newsletter *Impact*. Light beer, which accounted for a third of the market in 1990, should amount to half by 2013 because of them.

In addition to low cal, Anheuser-Busch has found that women respond to brews that are slightly sweeter, pack little aftertaste, and don't lead to gassiness or bloating. They want sophistication and elegance, not "chick beer" in pink bottles or to be the female equivalent of a fat, goofy, beer belly guy.

Of course, with men as the prime target, "beer and babes" ads are alive and well: Buxom twin beauties beat the drum for Coors, and in Miller Lite's "Catfight," two scantily clad gals tear at each other. (The ads have drawn notice but not sales.)

However, a new generation bows to those babes. An ad for Amstel Light, 45 percent of which is drunk by women, shows a babe opening a bottle with her teeth and spitting the cap across the bar. In a Miller Lite spot, a woman uses a rival's lesser quality brew to water her flowers. Coors Light set its fast-paced montage of a female karate black belt, firefighter, record executive, and dirt-biker to a remix of Tom Jones' "She's a Lady."

Even though brewers worry that using women in their commercials will repel men, Anheuser-Busch tries to get female lead characters in Bud Light spots "as central players, not enticements for men," says Bob Lachky, corporate vice president for brand management. In one spot, a woman shops laboriously for just the right greeting card for him. He picks one up for her as an afterthought while buying a six-pack at a convenience store. Anheuser-Busch runs Michelob Light spots on daytime TV—female territory—versus just prime-time and sports events.

Weaponry for Weapons

It is hard to imagine something more masculine than a gun. However, largely because manufacturers have redesigned their product and have used persuasive tactics, more and more women own them. Pro-gun organizations and the firearm industry have set their sights on women as an economic solution to declining sales. The National Rifle Association (NRA) also sought women members to soften its image of a group of chauvinistic rednecks.

Instead of the mainly rational, factual ads served to men, most of those pitched to women are ominous, sensational, and emotional. They show children and remind readers of rampant crime and their own vulnerability. Sarah Brady, chair of the Center to Prevent Handgun Violence, says that they exploit women's very legitimate fears. Gun lobby pamphlets harp on what it has determined women perceive as their greatest threat—rape. In a Second Amendment Foundation ad, a battered woman explains, "Last night I was raped. . . . Where were the police?" She reminds readers of the frequency of rape, robbery, and muggings "by thugs who don't think twice about hurting someone. You might be the next victim," she warns.

The industry's recruitment drive also involves presenting a gun as a tool of empowerment and a matter of choice. "I'm the NRA" gallery showcases accomplished women who have learned self-confidence from competitive shooting. And it argues against the "patriarchal" attempt to keep women from their rights and freedoms. In one ad, Detective Jeanne Bray says, "A gun is a choice women need to know more about and be free to make. And the NRA is working to ensure [that] the freedom of that choice always exists."

Peggy Tartaro, executive editor of *Women and Guns* magazine, claims that women have been falsely conditioned to believe that they are neither smart enough nor strong enough to handle a weapon effectively. "If you are smart enough to use a sewing machine or a word processor, you are smart enough to handle a firearm. And if you are strong enough to carry a man's groceries and a man's baby, you are strong enough to carry a man's gun."

The first manufacturer to aggressively court women was Smith & Wesson. In 1989, its catalog introduced the LadySmith with a choice of pearl or baby-blue grips that "manage to be elegant without sacrificing any of their practicality." Text positioned the handgun as a symbol of independence. "Gaining independence means assuming the responsibilities that go with it," the ad proclaimed.

Ads incited with such headlines as "You thought no one could fit in your back seat" and "Things that go bump in the night aren't always your imagination." In subsequent ads, a somber young woman is practice shooting under a headline that says, "What would mom think now?"

Colt Manufacturing ran an ad for its 9-mm pistol in *Ladies' Home Journal,* showing a mother tucking in her young daughter and Raggedy Ann doll under the headline, "Self-protection is more than your right . . . it's your responsibility." The ad described mom's duty as being "there for those who depend on you" and recommended "a dependable Colt semiautomatic pistol" to assuage guilt feelings.

However, guns, along with the fanny packs, bars and purses designed to conceal them, and hair bows that double as holsters are also presented as luxurious treasures. The LadySmith 38-caliber revolver nestles alongside a fur coat, single rose, and a brass lamp. Davis Industries describes its Saturday Night Specials as "Precious Possessions" and displays them beside a pearl necklace and diamond bracelet. New Detonics' Ladies Escort Series of 45-caliber handguns are available in purple with a gold-plated trigger, and Lorcin Engineering's Lady Lorcin is available in "designer Pearl Pink & Chrome finish." FIE Corporation's gold-plated Titan Tigress comes with a gold lamé carrying purse and ivorylike handle inscribed with a red rose.

Condoms

Not long ago, TV stations wouldn't run condom commercials, and pharmacists selling them in certain areas faced possible arrest. Now that sex has come out of the closet, so has almost-equal-opportunity preparedness for it. In the mid-1970s, women bought just 15 percent of the condoms sold nationwide. In 2002, they purchased 40 percent. (Women are also buying what experts estimate to be over a fourth of all the sex toys and paraphernalia sold.)

Their motivation: control and safety. Just as you wouldn't jump out of a plane without a parachute, as a 1996 Trojan print ad pointed out, you wouldn't set out on a possible sexual encounter without being able to call the shots and safeguard against pregnancy and disease.

As advanced technology enabled design innovations in condoms, marketers began playing up the pleasurable aspects associated with them. Trojan recently introduced Her Pleasure with "extra sensation for her most sensitive areas." An ad in women's magazines for a flavored condom urged women to "improve your taste in men." Others encouraged women to carry condoms in their purses. Then there was the female condom, Reality. The "soft, loose-fitting plastic pouch that lines the vagina," sells well overseas, but American women resist its looks, cost, squeakiness, and need to insert it.

Smoke and Mirrors

Cigarette companies have been blowing smoke at women since the 1920s, showing slim, attractive, athletic models and linking lighting up to success, social desirability, and independence. Early ads presented cigarettes as "torches of freedom" or urged women to "reach for a Lucky instead of a sweet" or to admire Chesterfield's monthly glamour gal (usually a fashion model or starlet such as Rita Hayworth, Rosalind Russell, or Betty Grable). By the mid-1930s, cigarette ads were so common that one for the Spud brand proclaimed that "to read the advertisements these days, a fellow'd think the pretty girls do all the smoking."

During the 1960s and 1970s, when one in three women smoked, tobacco companies developed such brands as Virginia Slims, Eve, Misty, and Capri just for them and advertised them as symbols of rebellion, independence, equality, and sophistication. "Slims" or "thins" played to their interest in staying svelte and managing stress. (In 1990, when R. J. Reynolds launched Dakota, it was lambasted for targeting "virile young women with little education who watch soaps and attend tractor pulls.")

In 1968, Virginia Slims told women they'd "come a long way, baby" and glorified images of thinness, independence, and gender equality. Later ads proclaimed, "It's a woman thing." More recent ones have implied that smoking is a way for women to "find your voice."

By 1974, the number of women smoking had rocketed. As reports of the hazards associated with smoking circulated, many quit. Tobacco companies fought to entice them back with new low-tar brands that, the companies implied, were softer and safer than regular cigarettes.

Today, 22 million American women smoke—and not just so-called female brands. Marlboro began in 1924 as a woman's cigarette with a red tip filter to mask lipstick stains and the slogan "Mild as May." However, the brand was gasping for air before Leo Burnett created the Marlboro Man, a symbol of idealized masculinity that oddly appealed to both men and women and made Marlboro the best-selling cigarette in the world.

Women are also puffing cigars. The George Sand Society, a cigar-smoking women's club, must have caught the attention of Consolidated Cigar Corporation, which introduced two specially shaped Don Diego stogies for women. Their ends are tapered to make them easier to light and more comfortable for the smaller female hand, says Executive Vice President Richard DiMeola.

As for those new cigarettes with perfumed scents, exotic flavors, names that include *slims* or *lights*, and packaging with watercolors and pastels—any guesses as to their market?

The Men's Room

You can still find a $1500 massage chair, a $600 chronograph Navy Seal dive watch, or a $10,000 suit of armor or remote-controlled submarine at Sharper Image. However, you also can find a lot more practical, affordable stuff such as hair dryers, nose-hair trimmers, and Ionic Breeze air purifiers.

Sharper Image is still king of high-end gadgets, but it has realigned its focus. For years its demographics were 75 to 80 percent male. More than likely the occasional female customer was there to buy a gift for a guy. Now women make up about 60 percent of Sharper Image shoppers, and they are buying more practical, affordable femme-focused products.

What Would Father's Day Be Without Women?

While Americans burn up the phone lines to commemorate Mom on Mother's Day, Father's Day isn't among the top five calling occasions. Nor is it a home run for flower vendors or even a tough day on which to get a restaurant reservation. However, it is a day when daughters remember their dads. In fact, they usually spend nearly twice as much as sons do for their dads, according to BizRate.com ($40 versus $23).

Women power has forced marketers of alcoholic beverages, condoms, weapons, and other "male" products to talk to—and even begin to cater to—the other, increasingly important, gender.

Part 2

How to Unclasp the Purse

15

Techniques for Selling to Women

Women pay attention to advertising. A recent study by RSC/The Quality Measurement Company, a market research firm specializing in measuring the effectiveness of commercials, found that women are 10 percent more likely to be persuaded by them than the population overall. Men are 16 percent less likely to be influenced.

The marketing challenge du jour is to communicate to women a "feels right" value proposition in a way that coaxes a smile of recognition and forges a bond. There are no rules on how to sell to women. Advertisers have been doing it successfully using various techniques to serve up strong selling propositions in fresh, engaging, and persuasive ways. There is no shortage of routes to reach women, but there are some guideposts to keep the journey on course.

1. Solve Her Problem

Women don't want *more* information; they want *useful* information that shows them how a product fits into their life and improves it. Compaq's advertising clicks with women because it demonstrates how technology lets them balance work and family. Kodak doesn't sell picture taking as much as the emotional benefit of love. Pantene isn't shampoo; it is the solution to dull hair. Cell phones aren't per-minute calling plans; they are a way for the family to reach women on the run. Clinique ads reject the distraction of too many choices by leading women to the one good thing: the clear, sure answer. And Dannon shows how its yogurt can help women snuggle into their favorite jeans or slinky party dress, says Daniel A. Stout, professor of communications at Brigham Young University.

Toyota shows Toyota owners as the stars, rather than the cars, "to show the customer how it's an elemental part of her life," said Joe McDonagh, formerly executive creative director at Saatchi. "People will read or watch only what's of particular interest to them—what has their story in it. We've got to show how we fit into the choices and decisions they've made."

In the past, ads for jeans promoted durability. This evolved into steamy, sensual, and strange campaigns with on-the-edge imagery. In 1987, Lee took a different, gentler tact, for its Relaxed Rider brand-that-fits positioning. It didn't need research to know that fit was the single most important criterion in picking jeans and that the process often was emotionally draining. Women try on 10 pairs of jeans on average before choosing one. Lee's ads identified the absurd but true-at-the-core rituals women go through in finding the right pair. Lee became both the solution and the brand that understands and empathizes. Women got it.

Savvy marketers know that solving women's problems often solves their own, fueling sales success. DYG's Madelyn Hochstein says that marketers can penetrate female barriers by communicating the product or service's benefits "as a tool to resolve key tensions." Convenience foods, for example, that feel like family values yet are simple and can be presented as something special do this well, she said.

In trying to increase women's purchasing of computer-related technology, marketers have abandoned macho power-revved bits and bites advertising of old to try to suggest how the tech products they are hawking will enhance women's lives and solve problems—as cell phones and beepers do.

2. Speak Her Language

When Eve sold Adam on the apple, she made the first sale without leave-behind brochures or Power Point presentations. Presumably she used speech (words) and body language (visuals) to persuade Adam of her vision.

Words are a marketers' dietary staple. They must be current and relevant. Jargon is never in fashion: Women wear clothes, not apparel. They want to know the price, not the price points. Last year's lingo is as dated as last year's shoe silhouette. (Birkenstock, known for its hippie sandals, is struggling to make its fashionable footwear hip today, but being rooted in the Woodstock generation is a big stigma to overcome.)

Sometimes what's unspoken causes a problem. If a deodorant ad claims that it is so effective that you need apply it only every *other* day, a man might think that this great because he's focused on the bottom line—effectiveness—says Joan Meyers-Levy, associate professor at the University of Chicago, who specializes in gender research. A woman, on the other hand, is likely to wonder what in heaven's name is in this stuff, and will it hurt me or the environment?

Language involves more than avoiding potentially troublesome words. It is choosing engaging, relevant words and arranging them artfully to connect a product, brand, or company with its customer— who they are now and who they want to be tomorrow. Microsoft spoke her language when it asked, "Where do *you* want to go today?"

Women want self-improvement, which is why Monster.com's exhortation to "Never settle" resonated with them. Yesterday's super-woman doesn't fly with today's balance-hungry mantra. Nowadays, status is attaining a comfort level with life, more control over things, and greater balance of work, family, and fun. Today's power broker doesn't sit in the back of a limo so much as in the front of a sport utility vehicle or hybrid, laptop or diaper bag at her side. (Indeed, former Secretary of Labor Robert Reich, professor at Brandeis University's Heller School for Social Policy and Management, sees a backlash against 24/7 and hears "a rising chorus of voices resolving to slow down." It is evident in the increasingly common return e-mail that says, in essence, "I'm on vacation and unavailable. Don't bother me.")

3. Make Her the Pilot

In a Woody Allen classic, a son asks his dad who's the boss in their family. Affronted, the man sputters that he is—mom makes the decisions, but he controls the TV remote control.

Marketers may laugh at this—all the way to the bank. Recognizing the innate truthfulness here, financial services no longer flaunt wealth or stature; they are presented as shrewd investments that give the investor control over her life. Likewise, technology doesn't just tout RAMs and pixels. It offers women less stress and more control. And women buy fragrance not so much to appeal to men as to improve their mood and sense of self.

Motorola moved from advertising single products to focusing on a mind-set of empowerment after a year of research convinced its marketing team that consumers want to be connected because they want to be in control, says Rich Darnaby, vice president and director of global brand management. Ads show how Motorola's products offer women the freedom "to take their worlds with them."

Mars understood the magic of getting their customers involved when it invited them to choose new colors for M&Ms. Crayola reached them, through their children, when it retired some shades and asked America to select replacements. Spiegel Catalog asked consumers to vote on future cover designs for its catalog. More and more, communication vehicles are two-way exchanges. Judy Moxhman, chief of PhaseOne, found that 43 percent of ads that fail to achieve above-average ratings did not build involvement with their target audience.

In 2002, Georgia-Pacific invited women to nominate a real hunk to go *mano a mano* with the fictional lumberjack on Brawny's packaging and in its ads since 1975. Four of the five finalists were firefighters, guys who displayed testosterone and tenderness. Along the way, the company discovered that women wanted strength, toughness, and dependability in cleaning supplies—not to worship the rescuer who got into those hard-to-reach corners. (In more recent spots, a woman grows her own powerful, muscled "Brawny arm" that tackles mammoth jobs expeditiously.)

To save costs, airlines have been testing to learn what food its customers will pay for. More than specific meal types, passengers are high on the idea of choice, even of the option of buying food. (They are choosing upscale-sounding ingredients and brand-name fare from such chains as TGI Friday's and Einstein Brothers but not the reheated mystery meats and diced vegetables they used to get with their ticket.)

Women may grouse about being the one who has to buy the gifts, but they secretly like the power it gives them in deciding which relationships to feed, says Mary Ann McGrath, an associate professor at Loyola University in Chicago.

Women's desire for more control of their lives boosted sales of caller ID and cell phones and convinced Verizon to bail on bigness and suggest cozy. "Big can suggest complexity. Big can suggest impersonal. Big can suggest a bully," admits Bruce Gordon, group president for retail services at the telecommunications giant. "People feel life is out of control and increasingly want what's small. It gives them a greater feeling of control and safety," says EURO RSCG chief strategist Marian Salzman. For this reason, Altoids never mentions that it is owned by Kraft nor Häagen Dazs that it's part of Pillsbury.

4. Respect Her, but For Heaven's Sake, Don't Pander

For years, marketers thought that the best way to sell to women was to make them feel inadequate (hence the unsightly dishwasher spots of old, for example). Women are still shown coming up short in some ways, but now they are onto this ploy and are less intimidated.

Women want to rely on strong, with-it brands, but their respect for the old is no longer absolute. Brand names must demonstrate repeatedly that they have earned their heritage and are up on the times. Otherwise, they get branded as the scent of their mothers (Chanel No. 5) or the car of their dads (Oldsmobile).

Marketers must earn respect, says Rebecca Maddox, president of Capital Rose, Inc., a consulting firm that focuses on training companies about the women's market. Ms. Maddox has seen brokers foolishly pitch life insurance only to the husband. Overlooking the wife as either a wage earner or decision maker is a cardinal mistake, she says.

Another blunder is making moms feel insecure about the minimal time they spend with their children. Moms want to maximize that connection and transform "kid time" from work to fun. (Rice Krispies did this by showing a mom and her daughter making its treats together as a bonding moment.) And moms are hungry for reassurance that they are doing a good job. Disney taps into this by presenting its magic kingdoms as educational as much as fun and fantasy. Hallmark also capitalized on that insight with its portrait of a boy whose mom finds a card from his teacher in his backpack. The lad shrugs it off as nothing, but she dredges out of him that he's been staying in at recess to play with a sick classmate who can't go outside. Mom is moved—especially by her son's insistence that "it's no big deal." Yet mothers everywhere know that it is: To have raised such a kind child defines a successful mom.

5. Make It Real

Stressed and busy, yes. Frazzled and bedraggled, no. Diana Holman, principal of WomanTrend, which teaches companies how to engage the second gender, says that marketers often portray women as caricatures of stressed-to-the-max maniacs who are out to lunch and out of control. In reality, most women feel that they have more on their plates than they would like but that they are coping.

And they welcome advertising that gives them permission to be real. Nike knew this years ago when it proclaimed that we're not perfect goddesses and never will be. The myth-breaking message helped its sales to women rocket. Whirlpool cleaned up with a headline announcing that washing clothes is a job with no end in sight. While "laundry is our life," the appliance maker conceded, "we know it's not yours." This ad signaled to women that Whirlpool recognized their priorities in an optimistic, we're-in-this-together way. This is in sharp contrast to the bug-eyed fascination with which women in ads once fawned over a bottle of Lysol.

Clara Peller, the raspy-voiced octogenarian, became an unlikely heroine in the infamous Wendy's "Where's the Beef?" commercial because she revealed the emperor-had-no-clothes truth. With less than a tenth of what rivals McDonald's and Burger King spent on ads, Wendy's implanted a slogan and sales message in women's minds—that those who demand quality will find it at this chain.

"Women, more so than men, like to see people in ads," says Judith Tingley, author of *Gender Sell: Selling to the Opposite Sex.* They especially want to see other women who are confident and naturally beautiful (which in today's world means diverse). "They want to see real women doing real things, having emotional, real-life experiences." This means that after years of picturing rail-thin 20-year-olds as Doctor Mom, the lady next door has landed the part.

Chances are that she is no spring chicken. In 1994, Lancome fired actress Isabella Rossellini for the unpardonable sin of turning 42. A few years later it hired the 58-year-old beauty Catherine Deneuve to represent its hair care products.

There are more women over age 40 now than ever before, so today's ads are full of laugh lines, rounder hips, and graying hair, with "graybes" (*gray* plus *babe*) such as Andie MacDowell, Julianne Moore, Jerry Hall, and Lauren Hutton surfacing everywhere. New York's Ford agency recently created a new division for models over age 40. In an editorial in a London newspaper, former fashion icon Twiggy (now in her fifties), chimed in, "After years of being sold antiwrinkle cream by teenagers, older models are finally stealing the limelight. It's about bloody time!"

Virtually every product now touts its authenticity. Politicians wear plaid flannel shirts to signal that they are just plain folks. (For "Real Thing" Coca-Cola it meant Penelope Cruz burping in an ad and Courtney Cox sparring with hubby David Arquette.) A Zogby poll found that more than twice as many people wanted to be known for being authentic as wanted to be considered smart or funny. And 61 percent would rather that their life mate be *real* than intelligent. This is part of the draw of "reality TV" personalities such as Evan Marriott (*Joe Millionaire*) and Trista Rehn (*The Bachelorette*) for KFC.

Guided by the insight that women's self-esteem derives largely from how they feel about their looks, Special K ads recently debunked the idea of an ideal body weight. Beauty, it argued, is more than a dress size; it is being strong and healthy and self-accepting. (As admirable as the sentiment is, it is fighting a Sisyphean battle. Kellogg's poll found that most women still strive for an "ideal" body weight and shape and that society has embraced one too.)

Way back in 1977, instead of fussing over the mechanics or technologies of picture taking, ads for Polaroid's One Step so-simple-to-operate camera that "even a woman can use it" featured the sparring, flirting celebrity endorsers James Garner and Mariette Hartley.

Their breezy battle of the sexes (which Hartley won handily) seemed so authentic that viewers believed that they really were married (and that the camera they touted *was* easier to use and more convenient than any other). For a time it was the best-selling camera in America.

6. Get to Her Buddies

If the way to a man's heart is through his stomach, the way to a woman's is through her friends and the families she cobbles together, with whom she shares her hopes, fears, time, energy, and secrets. The most sacred part of friendship, according to author Ann Patchett, are the contacts with no reason attached to them—not "to say, 'I'm having an affair' ... but to say, 'Why do I have four jars of pickles in my refrigerator?' It is the minutia, the willingness to offer up every detail, that marks the bond between women." Men, she noted, seem to prefer to bond over *something* and wouldn't follow a three-hour lunch with a "walk around looking in store windows as an excuse to just keep talking."

Women listen to their girlfriends—especially their opinions on how they look. Studies show that 43 percent of women highly value their friends' recommendations when it comes to purchases. They are also all ears to their friends' unspoken cues about what fits in their social set.

Coffee klatches and consciousness-raising groups of old have been supplanted by the contemporary community hives of book groups, investment clubs, and Botox parties, yet the need they meet is the same. Camp Jeep and the Saturn Reunion have tapped into this, offering opportunities to socialize and give owners a sense of connectedness. Timex ads are more about keeping friendships than about keeping time. Hallmark ("When you care enough to send the very best") pitches greeting cards as a way to cement relationships (and trump other card companies, the phone, *and* forgetfulness).

The old saw about telephone, telegraph, and tell a woman is true: Women share information. Research shows that women are three times as likely as men to hear about a product from their friends. If a woman is pleased, she tells others. If she isn't, she tells the world. Lynda Smith, consumer satisfaction consultant, says that 96 percent of women never complain to the company. They just never go back. And they mouth off to friends. The average woman delighted by a retailer tells 9 people about it; the average malcontent will spread the bad news to at least 20 people.

Verizon Wireless came in for a real tongue lashing over a Scrabble board recently as two women complained about persistent overcharges. The other two players resolved to avoid that carrier. And Neiman Marcus must surely rue that it added s $250 charge for its cookie recipe to one woman's lunch tab. After they ignored her persistent objections, she posted the recipe and rationale on the Web and in e-mail blasts to friends.

7. Aim for Her Gut

Women's intuition is more than the stuff of old wives' tales. It is a divining rod. Basic instinct has long been devalued, but marketers are coming to understand that it is a valuable resource that women bank on. "They *know* things by merging factual information with emotional tugs," says Madelyn Hochstein. Ads that sell a product's benefits alone rarely make the sale, no matter how superior those benefits are. Being the best is only the down payment on the price of admission. To complete the sale, women have to want to believe in the company and the product, she says.

This is why the shapes of bottles and the designs of labels on lots of products change—to make them seem current—but on products such as aspirin, they don't, because instinctually a woman is comfortable with a package that is the same as it was when she was a girl. A different package could lead her to think that the formulation has changed.

Similarly, carmakers play to women's visceral sensibilities by making sure that their doors deliver a whispered thud when they close (not a tinny sound) to signal strong, durable construction. And cake mixes still require that an egg be added because women instinctually feel that this means that they have baked from scratch.

Instinctual resistance to its "Rising" ads led United Airlines to ground them in 1999. They lacked the emotion of its long-running "Rhapsody in Blue" friendly skies theme. "We needed to make an emotional connection with consumers while reminding them that United is global, far reaching, friendly, and accessible," says John Kiker, vice president of advertising.

8. Make It Last

On the whole, women still look for commitment over one-night stands. While, generically speaking, men want cut-and-dried transactions to finalize fast, women want them to trigger relationships. Deborah Tannen, author of *You Just Don't Understand,* says, "Women speak and hear a language of connection and intimacy, while men speak and hear a language of status and independence."

Linda Denny, head of New York Life's Women's Initiative, says hit-and-run transactions or episodic consumer collisions don't build trust. "Women need to trust the person selling to them, and they want to know [that] the relationship will continue after the sale. Their loyalty often depends on maintaining a relationship, on building a bond."

This is why more companies are establishing consumer visitation rights far beyond 800 numbers and Web-site feedback. *Everyone* from hair salons to car washes offers frequency flyer/buyer/renter cards to engender loyalty and move beyond a deal to a relationship. Women like that in addition to rewarding them discounts, supermarkets that track their buying habits offer them relevant specials. They like the dental hygienist calling to schedule an appointment for a cleaning. And they enjoy receiving a dealer's follow-up letter after they have bought a car. It soothes postpurchase doubt, what marketers call *cognitive dissonance,* and reassures her that she's chosen wisely.

9. The Pause That Refreshes

In 1972, when L'Oreal launched Preference hair color, it aimed to justify its premium price by convincing women to value themselves— and therefore pay a bit more. Its four little words—"Because I'm Worth It"—made for a legendary ad campaign that has since evolved into "Because you're worth it." Carol Hamilton, president of L'Oreal Paris Brand, says that the campaign "elevates a woman's confidence and self-esteem." At the same time it connects their bolstered self-images to L'Oreal's products, making them the pause that refreshes.

L'Oreal's line opened the floodgates. Other companies such as Neutrogena now urge women to "be free to spend more on yourself," and good-taste gurus such as Martha Stewart and Emeril Lagasse peddle prestige to the masses. This hits on an elemental truth: Women like to be cosseted and coddled.

This is why they will pay $5.49 for a pound of Horizon organic butter or $3 for a small container of Fresh Samantha carrot/orange juice, why AT&T's one-rate USA plan "encourages you to indulge," and why in addition to the kitchen and bathroom, the laundry room has come out of the closet—or gloomy basement—and gone showcase sumptuous. Clothes-care appliances have gone high-tech and high priced—like $1500-plus front-loading washers from Miele and Maytag.

Spas, aromatherapy, and bath and body products have all taken off because women love to be pampered. Other marketers have borrowed from this well, suggesting that their products soothe and satisfy. Fragrance ads used to be about getting the guy; now they are about savoring pleasure. Origins calls a lotion Peace of Mind. Pepsico serves up Zen Blend and Karma Tranquilities. According to *Publishers Weekly*, almost 600 new spiritual and religious guides were published in summer 2003. Commercials for Green Tea Therapy with such words as *healing* and *inner light* suggest that peace of mind has become the ultimate Holy Grail.

Club Med had it right a few years back when it proclaimed itself the antidote to civilization. General Foods' International Coffees are not so much instant beverages as a destress zone in a harried day. And cars with heated seats and "memory" that recalls climate settings and instantly adjusts to the driver's preferred seat position tap into this same desire.

But there's more to good times than pampering. There's merrymaking, highlighted by Halloween, erstwhile a moment of mysticism and magic and now the fastest growing holiday and one actively embraced by one in three women. Apple built a cult and women's loyalty by making them feel part of an elite creative corps *and* by celebrating fun. Its colorful iMacs made a functional product flippant.

Food is about more than nutrition. It is about pleasure and gratification and pigging out. We may be skittish about calories and cholesterol one minute and indulging in fats and fun the next. Weary of being warned away from certain temptations, women are flaunting the rules and sinking their teeth into undercooked red meat and other forbidden fruits.

10. Lay Out a Safety Mat

Headlines on everything from *Listeria* to "pfiesteria," phone call monitoring to credit card fraud, and Bin Laden to biological weapons have made us nervous wrecks. We are living in a virtual spook house, with frights on each horizon. Take germs, for example. Ninety-six percent of women admit they are anxious about them (up from 77 percent in 1995). Bottled water sales in this country soared 144 percent in a decade, and 73 percent of women use antibacterial liquid soap.

Cyber Dialogue analyst Idil Cakim says that fear propels nearly 7 of every 10 women online to go offline to complete a transaction. (On the other hand, some women order drugs online to ensure anonymity the way the old drug store used to wrap sanitary napkins in brown paper.) More restaurants situate their kitchens in the open so that diners can see what goes on. Just 19 percent of us *don't* worry about our privacy, says Dr. Alan Westin, president of Privacy & American Business. Indeed, Yankelovich Partners President J. Walker Smith says that an undercurrent of anxiety is the "new normalcy."

The serpent seduced Eve by playing to her fear of missing out. Fear is a powerful motivator. Sylvan Learning Centers and the *Princeton Review* have frightened parents into enrolling little Matthew for fear that he won't get into Harvard without them. Flonase warns that "What you don't know about Clarinex, Zyrtec, and Allegra may cost you." In Prudential ads, a middle-aged dad worries about how he can provide for his kids. And because Bill is scared of termites, a young couple resorts to preposterous extremes, including living in an all-cement home (instead of calling Terminex).

While research shows that weak fear appeals work better than strong ones, successful ads need do more than just alarm an audience. They must provide just enough relevant, reputable, and credible information to get people to act, not overreact. If ads are too scary, people become paralyzed, unbelieving, or uninterested.

It's not that women go through life holding on to hand rails so much as that they don't like risks without benefit. Protective products help them to avoid that. Volvo's marketing chassis is safety. In ads, owners relate how they walked away from serious accidents. Samples and money-back guarantees also reduce risk, although, oddly, they work better with new beauty products than with pills, Roper found. Jann Leeming, executive editor of *About Marketing & Women,* says that the best way to market cars and computers to women is to focus on warranties and service reputation. With men, it's to advertise price, features, and performance.

Women warm to restaurants that stand behind a meal, a wrinkle remover that promises to remove facial creases, and grocers who claim that the customer is always right. They see clearly stated, hassle-free guarantees as a way to purchase peace of mind. Despite its heftier cost, women continue to use FedEx because of its ironclad assurance never to be late. Avon Anew comes with a timeline guarantee. Credit cards routinely offer free extended protection on purchases made with them. Now, more than one in four homes sold comes with a contract, according to the National Home Warranty Association. Automakers use extended warranties to offset consumer doubts about reliability, says George Peterson, president of the research firm Autopacific. Hyundai pioneered this in 1999, promising to pay for bumper-to-bumper repairs for up to 10 years or 100,000 miles and to provide free roadside assistance for 5 years.

Warranties have become an integral part of many marketing programs. If, for any reason, you didn't love your Jaguar, you could return it for a full refund. Not 100 percent satisfied? Xerox will replace machines for free up to 3 years from the purchase date. Still have cavities even though you have brushed with Crest for 6 months? Swap the toothpaste for your money back. Women like the offers but don't always take the company up on them. Although 61 percent of men and 68 percent of women faithfully send in warranty cards according to *Adweek*, many never bother collecting.

11. Make It Easy

"Teenagers and techies will put up with plenty of aggravation to get technology to work. Mom will not. Her life is too complicated," said Tim Woods, vice president of the Internet Home Alliance, a consortium that includes Sears, IBM, and Hewlett-Packard, among others, which sponsored an experiment involving networked appliances. A futuristic oven, for example, both cooks and refrigerates food and can be controlled remotely by cell phone or personal computer.

Women yearn for simplicity. Four of five claim to be actively seeking ways to streamline their lives. Many admit to feeling overwhelmed by their possessions and eager for a less materialistic life. Even Martha Stewart's fledgling magazine, *Everyday Food,* sounds like a convert. *Fast* and *easy* scream from the cover; inside, a salmon recipe calls for 5 minutes of prep time, and a fettuccine Alfredo lists three ingredients.

Eighty-three percent of women have abandoned their cybercart in frustration because a Web site was too hard to use, according to Rob LoCascio, chief executive officer of LivePerson.com. Women want sites organized by how they think, not how the company has organized its product line. LivePerson.com, which connects consumers to a company representative in real time, has mushroomed because "women want to know whether that sweater in medium in forest green is in stock," says LoCascio.

The search for simplicity has spawned such successes as Revlon's extended-wear Color Stay lipstick and Cover Girl's Marathon line. Now biotechnologists are working on fragrances that don't fade for 7 hours, making reapplication unnecessary.

Saturn intentionally made its cars easy to operate and maintain with clear labels directing where to pour the wiper fluid and how to change the oil. Ditech.com and Lending Tree chirp about fast it is to apply for a home equity loan—and faster even to get accepted. "We'll even come to you for the signing," says one ad.

Organizational gizmos from Rubbermaid, Hold Everything, California Closets, and the like also benefit from the simplicity crusade.

12. Make It a Deal

Instead of focusing on the most comfortable seats in the sky, recent American Airlines ads focus on the folks it hopes will sit in them. In TV commercials, various travelers describe how they scored more legroom for less money.

Today, women increasingly pride themselves on how little, not how much, they paid. Target hit the bull's-eye with its "discount chic," whereas "Some people get it. Some people get it for less" has worked for T.J. Maxx. Star Jones, the self-proclaimed "Diva of Stylish Shoes" and cohost of ABC's *The View*, reinforces the "Look smart; Payless" theme. "She's comfortable wearing Payless shoes with a $3000 dress," says John Haugh, head of marketing at Payless ShoeSource. "Women today want value, but they don't want to be a season behind." Roper found that 61 percent of women only buy on sale (versus 49 percent of men). And 70 percent claim a deep satisfaction in finding a "good deal."

What could be better than an incentive offer? Americans have gotten addicted to them, says Andy Turton, president of the North American Division of NFO Automotive, a marketing information company. For one in three car buyers, 0 percent financing helped overcome fears and worries in the post-9/11 climate, he says.

Multiple benefits also sweeten a deal. Women want it all in a single bottle—shampoo plus conditioner; the duo eyeshade in one stroke; the hair dryer with five removable attachments; a cream that moisturizes, reduces wrinkles, and improves skin quality overall. In this multitasking world, the Rembrandt three-in-one whitening gel, mouthwash, and anticavity brand is "the oral care equivalent of walking and chewing gum at the same time," said Bette Light, spokeswoman for Rembrandt parent Den-Mat Corp.

The International Mass Retail Association says that women pay more attention to coupons, promotions, and contests than men do, but only one in five is interested in marketing games.

13. Cause and Effects

A long time ago, before "policy" became the fifth P of traditional marketing (along with product, pricing, place, and promotion), women looked for the union label. Now they are seeing the pink ribbon and putting their money where their missions are. If the price is equal, two-thirds of women (but only 15 percent of men) are likely to switch brands based on a good cause, according to Roper. They go out of their way to buy from companies that support causes dear to them. A recent Cone Communications' study found that women most want to support local projects that affect kids and the environment. And they value that "Made in the USA" label more than men do, according to the International Mass Retail Association. In a world of parity products, Avon's corporate benevolence to breast cancer sufferers has helped differentiate it from its rivals.

Cause-related marketing mushroomed in the early 1980s when American Express launched a national program to restore Ellis Island and the Statue of Liberty and then launched the successful "Share Our Strength" program to prevent hunger. Now Starbucks promotes its relationship with CARE, Nike supports Boys and Girls Clubs, and Nabisco underwrites the World Wildlife Fund. McDonald's earns points for its Ronald McDonald House, Home Depot gains from its community-development initiatives, and Pizza Hut has a hit with its "Book It" literacy program.

14. Segment—Or Not

In an AT&T ad a few years ago, a daughter asks her mom why she works. "So I can buy you video games and roller skates," Mom replies. This hit the truth button for some moms, but others bridled at her values and resented that she had chosen such fripperies (versus working for something important like paying the mortgage) over staying home with her brood.

Edgy ads *can* polarize. As a result, many ads targeted to moms have become sanitized, vanilla clichés, says Denise Fedewa from the Leo Burnett agency. Marketers need to choose who they are talking to and accept that their appeal might alienate others, she says.

Women are not a homogeneous group. Individually, in fact, each woman is many people in one, different personalities on different occasions. (A Calvin Klein ad once summed it up: "I'm just a simple complicated woman.") Juggling multitaskers, they are usually the household command center, mediator, appointment maker and taker, and chief cook and bottler washer. Marketing to one of these roles means missing all the others.

Marketers often define and segment women by their lifestyle, and for good reason: Twenty-year-olds read fashion magazines nearly seven times more than 58-year-olds. Convenience is a bigger draw for working moms than company reputation, and while gen-X woman like entertainment and pampering, retirees are more interested in attentive sales help and "silver" discounts.

LeoShe identified four mother "types": modern-day June Cleavers, who tend to be white, rich, educated, and fulfill themselves by mothering; tug-of-war moms, who have jobs but little income and a lot of guilt and anger that they are not June Cleavers; strong shoulders moms, mainly young, single, self-sufficient, and making the best of it; and mothers of invention, who share parenting with their mate, are big users of technology, and have flexible work arrangements.

Car companies, with the help of psychologists, psychiatrists, anthropologists, hypnotists, and dream analysts, have sliced and diced prospects into more than 50 demographic and lifestyle microcosms—with names such as "Blue Blood Estates," "New Ecotopia," "Young Literati," and "Shotguns and Pickups" to aim messages at. Sports and muscle cars, for example, known in Motown as "vehicle Viagra," strike a different "emotional pulse" than a Honda Civic or Toyota Corolla—pitched to those who pride themselves on their practicality.

Marketers who understand their target's life don't have to show that life in their ads—just that they understand it, says Burnett's Fedewa. The hard part is figuring out what is most compelling to that audience and how to express it. For example, if you are selling brooms to "mothers of invention," convey the idea that your broom picks up dirt better than any other broom.

Not segmenting also can work. "Money is green, not pink or blue," says Randall Miller, executive vice president of T. D. Waterhouse, which eschews gender-specific ads. Levi's also jettisoned its "Jeans for women" campaign, feeling that the era of gender marketing has passed. Deloitte & Touche's Cindy Sobieski advises talking to women "in the way that they will know you want them without saying *women*." Whatever you do, however, don't make it pink.

15. Tread Softly and Forget About the Big Stick

Quick, name a public place without advertising. Churches, mosques, and synagogues; national parks; and the American flag—it's a short list getting shorter. Ads and product placements have invaded books, films, and music videos; public restrooms; cabs and buses; elevators; and the skies.

With 500 channels, DirecTV, blogs, and TiVo, mass media has been demassed. In 1995, it took three TV commercials to reach 80 percent of 18- to 49-year-old women. In 2000, just 5 years later, it took 97 ads to reach the same group, according to Willard Bishop Consulting. "Short of being embroiled in a scandal," concludes ad agency Doremus in a recent newsletter, "it's almost impossible to get your name in enough channels to build substantial awareness."

Therefore, companies are taking different promotional steps to connect their brands to consumers. Instead of full-frontal assaults, many are gently surrounding their targets, supplementing traditional magazine, TV, billboard, and newspaper ads; Web sites; coupons; and direct-mail pitches with fresh marketing schemes—they call it ambient media—to win prospects over. They are imbedding the products in James Bond movies (the audience is half female, says Revlon) and movie trailers, music videos, fitness events, golf courses, scavenger hunts, sampling binges, school tours, even on banana peels.

Helpful brand ambassadors hand out dog biscuits to human companions and binoculars to concert goers to "connect AT&T with people," said John Palumbo, president of experiential marketing agency DVCX, NY. Restaurants leave menus with special offers for moms at day-care centers. To launch Nivea Visage Q10 Wrinkle Control Cream, the company distributed samples to female DJs with strong female audiences—to try and talk about.

Framed ads for Noxzema products, Sony Music, and Salem cigarettes are tacked inside bathroom stall doors in bars. Ads for movies have flashed on automatic teller machine screens and "floor billboards" at supermarkets. Skippy Peanut Butter carved its ad into the sand at a New Jersey beach. Hyatt Hotel bellhops pass out

"HyattPalooza," mints with travel deals. Tampax has staged nightclub parties to introduce its new Pearl brand.

At more than 20 events, including state fairs and the Super Bowl, Procter & Gamble set up immaculate outdoor bathrooms complete with running water, wallpaper, faux wood floors, Charmin toilet paper, Safeguard hand soap, Pampers changing tables, and Bounty paper towels to provide something of a cheek-to-cheek comparison with the customary Porta-Potties. "People don't think much about toilet paper, so to get them to focus and understand the benefits of Charmin Ultra, you really need for them to try it," says brand manager Diane Cercle, who runs "Pottypalooza."

As consumer products' seer Faith Popcorn has said, "Market to her peripheral vision, and she will see you in a whole new light."

16

Humor: Tickle Me Elmo

Testimonials, demonstrations, side-by-side comparisons, and emotional pitches all can attract a woman's attention. So can going for the giggle. "At least a third of commercials now are funny—or attempt to be," says Cliff Freeman, chairman of Cliff Freeman & Partners, the agency that created "Pizza, Pizza" for Little Caesar's and "Yeah, We Got That" for Staples.

In some sense, the marketplace is a popularity contest. People choose products they like. If they like the advertising, they are more likely to like the product—and vice versa. We love to laugh, and therefore, we opt for ads that tickle our funny bones and lighten our moods.

Amusing advertising makes a product fun. "Without fun advertising, fun food becomes just food," says Mike Hogan, marketing director at Frito Lay. Funny ads can make a brand more comfortable, informal, and inviting, he says. We are exposed to over 3000 messages a day, but only those that cut through the clutter get remembered. Humor does that, "seducing" the consumer enough to make her take notice and bringing down barriers of resistance.

Humor also can make cash registers ring. "If you can share a smile with someone, you've made a friend," said Arthur Bijur, president of the Freeman agency. "Humor works because it warms people up and relaxes them. It creates connection, opens a window to get a message in." Little Caesar's surged from third to a strong runner-up to Pizza Hut because of its wacky ads. One showed a zany pizza counterman fashioning an origami pterodactyl from a pizza box; another showed the rigors at a boot camp for training pizza deliverers. Cathy Davis, Discover Card's vice president of brand management, says that lighthearted ads make a brand more credible and demonstrate "that you believe [that] your customers are intelligent and that you value their time."

Humor in advertising is also something of a sine qua non. "People want something back. If they're going to let you try to sell them, they want to be entertained," said Ted Sann, chief creative officer at the BBDO agency.

Yet going for the guffaw can be perilous. Some topics, such as cancer, are no laughing matter. If a product is very important, you should tell people important things about it, says Jay Schulberg, formerly creative chief of Bozell. Responding to a message by slapping your knees and spewing milk from your nose trivializes it, and the potential to backfire is big. "It's not funny if you turn people off . . . and if it's not funny, that's what you do," warns Schulberg. And what's funny to one person isn't to another. Wendy's 'Where's the Beef?' was hilarious—if you weren't old and didn't want to be presented as crotchety. One woman's meat is another's repulsion.

And then many people have *no* sense of humor. Studies suggest that men react better to flip ads than women and whites better than African-Americans. Audiences can't "get it" if they aren't in the know. For an ad in which Stevie Wonder says, "Before I'll ride with a drunk, I'll drive myself," to work, it is necessary to know that he is blind.

"Further, if the only thing viewers remember is the joke, by definition, you've failed," says Schulberg. Wit, on the other hand—demonstrated by the classic Volkswagen ads of old (think "Lemon")—makes the marketing proposition the star. It gives the consumer a sense of achievement when she gets the pun, helping her remember the brand. Humor must be brand- or feature-specific, with the joke connected to the product in some way, focusing on some product benefit to be effective.

Funny ads can boost agency morale and the client's reputation, win awards, and interest the kids, but this is no sure-fire way to build brand retention, housewife confidence, or understanding of the product benefits, warns marketing expert Dr. Jack Kopf. And the big catch: The funnier they are, the sooner they irk. Who wants to hear the same joke a dozen times?

Direct-mail pitches rarely use humor. (One notable exception—the political magazine *The Nation* gets guffaws and checks.) Direct-response experts believe that humor is a good attention-getting opener but not a closer. The relationship between gaining attention and actually marketing is one of stopping somebody on the street and actually selling them something. "It's an introductory proposition," says Herschell Gordon Lewis, direct-mail consultant.

More and more marketers, however, are discovering that even macabre humor closes sales. Alliance Capital proved the old saw, "If it's my money, it's not funny" to be toothless bunk with ads that showed retirees, who failed to plan adequately, paying the price, comically, of course. (E-Trade's monkey saw and did the same.) FedEx implanted in our minds that it, like death and taxes, is absolutely positively to be counted on with more than a decade of side splitters starting with a fast-talking executive who expresses how FedEx helps us keep up with the fast-paced world.

And more "serious" categories are opting to go droll. HealthOne shows a young couple dwelling on frivolous decisions such as how to position a chair and the right shade of huckleberry and contrasts this with the amount of time they devote to picking their hospital. HealthOne didn't resort to smiling nurses, new technology, or screeching ambulances to reach 25- to 55-year-old women, says Marketing Vice President Linda Kanamine. Humor made this stand out and added a bit of accessibility to the category, she says.

Research suggests that funny ads work best for familiar, "low involvement" products that are bought frequently and are low in price, such as food. High-involvement products such as cars involve a lengthier, more intense thought process, with customers looking for hard facts and information up front.

Done right, humor can be a marketer's best medicine, says Cliff Freeman. "Because it means pleasure, people watch it more avidly. Nobody can ever be bored into buying anything."

17

Sex or Sensibility?

Sex sells. It has been used to push everything from whitening tooth-pastes to blue jeans to red sedans to translucent condoms. Sometimes it is delivered with a come-hither smirk or wink ("Nothing comes between me and my Calvins"). Other times it is more direct or Freudian. Years back, a single episode—when an attractive woman borrowed coffee from her handsome, single neighbor—percolated into a 12-part serial romance for Taster's Choice.

"Sex is stopping power," says Andrew Hayman, executive vice president at Publicis. "It breaks the message out of the clutter. And associating a product with pleasure propels purchase," he says.

Sex has been used in TV advertising since the medium began. In the mid-1960s, a sexy blonde invited men to "Take it off, take it all off" for Noxzema shaving cream. Auto ads routinely featured skimpily clad models draped on the car as part of the "buy the car, get the bird" mind-set. Jovan had to recut its "What Is Sexy" cam-paign in 1987 because censors thought wriggling toes suggested fore-play. Even conservative Coca-Cola slipped here a few years back in a Diet Coke spot where women ogled a hunky construction worker to the tune of "I Just Wanna Make Love to You."

"The job of a commercial is to get viewers, especially prospects for the product, to say, 'Holy cow, I've never seen anything like that in my life,'" says Chanel, Inc., President Arie Kopelman. Chanel has been doing that for years—mothering one of the most famous sensual commercials of all time. In a 1979 ad for Chanel No. 5, languorous beauty Catherine Deneuve tosses her stiletto shoe into a pool and arches rapturously as an airplane's shadow floats above. An Adonis slices into the water in a perfect dive, retrieves the shoe, and suggestively emerges from under water between the V of her knees. Interpreters had a heyday decoding the supposed Freudian symbolism.

Victoria's Secret brought men into its fold with a parade of vamps gyrating down a runway on a Super Bowl right before Valentine's Day. Oddly, women also were turned on by it.

"Women are surprisingly more accepting about sex in ads than men are," says Kim Barnes, senior partner of strategic planning and research at the former Bozell Worldwide. Its national survey revealed that only 24 percent of women feel turned off by ads that blatantly use sex, compared with 45 percent of men. In fact, twice as many women as men (44 versus 21 percent) think that showing sexy women in ads helps to sell products—with older women likeliest to agree.

How to explain this seeming enigma? Barnes thinks that women have become accustomed to marketers pounding away at them and that they are far more understanding and forgiving of "fringe" strategies. Lisa Bennett, communications director of the National Organization of Women Foundation, thinks that it's that "images of models in push-up bras with 'please ravage me' eyes have become the wallpaper of our lives . . . so commonplace that most people fail to even notice it anymore."

Overall, Barnes says that women feel that sexuality or sensuality fits with categories such as fashion and fragrance and that they have grandfathered acceptance of it in beer ads. However, when it is used to sell something unrelated, say, a video game to teen boys, it is a turnoff.

Women often see beyond the sex ad to a deeper level of romance and love. So much of advertising is "aspirational" that they "see the jiggle and fantasize themselves in the situation," she says.

More than two-thirds of women—68 percent—say that they identify with the women they see in ads. Men may object to sexy ads as a PC reflex, having been taught that they demean women, she says.

Women also may be letting sexual innuendos slide because no one is particularly noticing them, says Rod Smith, senior consultant at Detroit-based MORPACE International, Inc. When his research firm surveyed advertising recall, sex-stacked spots scored poorly. "We're seeing that people are fed up with explicit sexual messages used to sell products," says Tim Gibson, executive vice president and creative director at Freedman, Gibson & White, Inc. He traces people's prejudice against va-va-va-voom advertising to the Clinton-Lewinsky shenanigans when people became oversaturated with sex. The "reality" matchmaker shows are more about the titillation of surprise (Joe was no millionaire) than sex.

America's fatigue with sex in advertising may explain why many marketers are using female sexuality as a source of strength instead of vulnerability, says Sherrie Patel, vice president and senior planner at Leo Burnett and cofounder of Leoshe, an agency unit created to cater to women.

When the "Charlie girl" goosed the guy, it was flirtation in which she was in control. A *Vanity Fair* lingerie ad a few years back featured older women in sexual poses but with copy talking about wisdom and life experience. In summer 2003, for its Air Zoom Spiridon shoes, Nike zoomed in for a prolonged close-up of runner Kathryn Martin's derriere. But instead of titillation, we get self-satisfaction. "See that?" she asks. "That is 51 years old, and it can run a 5:08." Her face with its laugh lines and graying hair is that of a middle-aged woman.

"Rather than ignore sex, smart advertisers are using it as a source of personality and strength, not treating women as objects or playthings," Patel says. "Sexiness per se doesn't offend; it's positioning a woman as an object that's objectionable."

18

Star Power or
Girl Next Door?

Diva Celine Dion was the fourth biggest earner among music industry artists in 2002, behind the Dave Matthews Band but ahead of Eminem. In 2003, Chrysler Group and Coty Beauty bet big that she could sell cars and gels.

Chrysler committed a queen's ransom to engage the chanteuse. In an ad for its Crossfire, she crooned, "I Drove All Night." In one for its Town & Country minivan, she and her toddler son René coddled as passengers to her hit, "Have You Ever Been in Love?" In a spot for the Pacifica, the vocalist rehearsed a cappella.

And Coty used everything from traditional ads to guerilla-marketing efforts to launch its Celine Dion collection of lotions, gels, and scents—including fragrance machines at Dion's "A New Day" show and the gift of her CD with a beauty purchase.

Despite their high hopes—Chrysler Marketing Communications Director Bonita Stewart said that Dion "brings sophistication, refinement, romance, and passion to the brand with an appeal that crosses ethnic lines," and Coty Beauty President Eric Thoreux called her "the ultimate romantic person but not sugary romantic"—the golden voice fell on deaf ears. Women in chat groups groused doubts that the diva ever drives herself and were indignant that the French Canadian sang "land where my fathers died" during the Super Bowl.

Celebrities can crack through ad clutter and interest women in a brand. They have long been used to symbolize the most relevant strategic idea in a category. Dozens of high achievers whose names were better known than their faces used the American Express card to get star treatment. Paloma Picasso, for example, packed it to be as recognizable as her jewelry creations. Coca-Cola couldn't change the world or heal Mean Joe Greene's injuries, but it brought a smile to Mr. Tough Guy, the Pittsburgh Steelers' glowering defensive lineman.

Duchess of York Sarah Ferguson (unkindly termed the "duchess of pork") revitalized Weight Watchers, and infamous tax victim Willie Nelson parodied his run-ins with the Internal Revenue Service to show how taxpayers can benefit from H&R Block's Double Check Challenge. "We didn't pick Willie just because he was a celebrity but because there was something in his past that connected him to our message," said Karl Ploeger, vice president at H&R Block. With tongue in cheek, fashion designer Marc Jacobs tapped actress Winona Ryder for ads after she wore his outfits to her shoplifting trial in 2002.

Pepsi, which long ago hitched its wagon to star power, recently replaced fading pop star Britney Spears with Beyonce Knowles of Destiny's Child to show that it is the choice of a new generation. Coke recruited actresses Penelope Cruz and Courtney Cox Arquette; the latter's husband, actor David Arquette; Tour de France winner Lance Armstrong; boxing great Muhammad Ali; and Winston Cup champion Tony Stewart because they are "comfortable with being themselves," says Esther Lee, Coke's chief creative officer. Revlon uses Halle Berry in ads linked to the Bond flick to reinforce its "Unforgettable Women" positioning.

Val Kilmer shills for Nikon, Ving Rhames for Radio Shack, and Sarah Michelle Gellar, Jessica Biel, Kristin Kreuk, and Katie Holmes for a slew of beauty products. Alec Baldwin is the voice of Chevy trucks, and Jeff Goldblum is bedazzled for iMac. Can you recall the last time you saw Jason Alexander without a bucket of chicken?

Buick uses Tiger Woods, and new mom Brooke Shields, who started her endorsement career at 11 months of age as the Ivory Snow baby, is now pitching Bright Beginnings baby formula. Heavyweight George Foreman made Salton grills sizzle; women find him cuddly and believable. Dead actors also have gotten into the act. In 1996, John Wayne pitched Coors, although he had died 17 years earlier. Fred Astaire danced with a Dirt Devil vacuum cleaner. Humphrey Bogart flogged Thomasville Furniture. The list goes on and on.

Using celebrities in ads is about borrowing equity. Nike shoes feel better because of the star athletes from Michael Jordan on down who wear them. Wheaties cereal is good because Barry Bonds eats it. Supposedly, affection for a celebrity rubs off on the product. While only 16 percent of viewers could remember the name of a product in an average commercial, Starch Research found that adding a star could double that identification.

However, using real stars is risky. They cost, they fade, and they can overpower the message and spread themselves too thin. Ace Hardware found itself in a vise when Suzanne Somers bared it all. Chrysler hit a celebrity pothole in 2002 when it linked to now-indicted Martha Stewart. Then there's Kobe Bryant.

"Celebrities can overshadow a brand—or their troubles can," says Kelly O'Keefe, chief executive officer of Emergence Brand Labs.

Jaded consumers know that celebrities do it for the money. Anthropologist Jane Goodall took heat for appearing in a spot for HBO in which she and her primate friends were glued to the movie channel—when there was no TV in the bush. If you cast a celebrity such as Jennifer Lopez as the Pine Sol lady, "you'd know she never used the product," says Jill Murray, copywriter at DDB. Actress and comedian Diane Amos has held that job since 1993. She "seemed like someone viewers would believe used the cleanser," Murray adds.

The ability of celebrities to convince women has declined steadily since 1987 when Michael Jackson and Cybill Shepherd admitted that they didn't drink Pepsi or eat beef. Only 3 percent of women say that they would try a new product based on a celebrity's recommendation, according to Yankelovich Partners. Word of mouth from a girlfriend carries much more weight. And studies show that just 15 percent of viewers, without prompting, correctly associate most celebrities with the products they are paid to tout. Recall of animals such as the Budweiser Clydesdales is considerably higher.

With so many stars now cluttering the firmament, fewer commercials shine as brightly. This gave Alltel a bright idea. Its "You got that right" campaign poked fun at its cellular service rival's reliance on celebrities—to show it uses common sense. Academy Award winner Catherine Zeta-Jones pitches for T-Mobile and James Earl Jones for Verizon, actress Joan Cusack stands in for U.S. Cellular, and actor Dennis Franz speaks for Nextel Communications. In one Alltel spot, members of a boy band ("worth every million"), singing praises to "Super Massive Wireless," are hoisted by ropes in a ludicrous parody of stage antics. An irked consumer wonders why they don't spend money on making his phone work better, and Alltel jumps in to say that it is doing just that.

In this oversaturated media environment, some marketers say that we are celebrity-pitched out. Subway skipped celebrities and used real-life dieter Jared Fogle to boost credibility. Subway spokesman Les Winograd says that the Jared ads succeeded because he is not a celebrity. "Research indicates [that] women are much more concerned with health than [with] seeing celebrities," said Andrea Saia, vice president of marketing for Equal sweetener, which dropped famous women for vignettes of real ones.

Since 1995, moreover, instead of talking heads or spokesman actor Peter Strauss, "regular guy" Jerry Looby has been getting lawn-envious neighbors to follow his lead for Scotts' Turf Builder lawn and garden products. "The whole idea is to say to consumers that this isn't such a big, complicated thing," says Lee Reichart, vice president for advertising. Scotts' research shows that women account for 70 percent of garden care purchases, but men buy most lawn care products.

Famous people and fashion houses have been coupling since Barbara Stanwyck endorsed Blackglama in the 1970s and Debbie Harry did Gloria Vanderbilt in the 1980s. More recently, Jennifer Lopez hawked Louis Vuitton; Cate Blanchett, Donna Karan;

Christina Aguilera, Versace; and Madonna, she of the double-barreled Gaultier brassiere, pitched the prewashed khakis and crisp white shirts of The Gap. The nation's largest specialty apparel retailer is also banking on hip-hop rap star Missy Elliott to make it chic a gain.

By choosing the 44-year-old yoga-practicing renegade fashionista mom, The Gap hoped to sell Capri's to America. The Gap's customers reflect a wide swath of the country: Madonna with her wide range from picture books to porn covers the waterfront.

Picking this pop icon was a controversial step, however. Some say that she is passé for young people and has too much baggage for older ones. Others consider her synonymous with cool and style.

Meanwhile, after a short span, Chrysler decided that Celine Dion was not meeting its goal of selling more cars and minivans without huge rebates. Marketing Vice President Jim Schroer, who called Dion the perfect representative for Chrysler's "path to premium" positioning, resigned. Dion herself all but disappeared from Chrysler ads, although her music does go on.

19

Cobrand or No Brand

Kids encouraging mom to buy broccoli? This is part of the fun of a 2003 commercial in which a masochistic young girl confides to Mickey Mouse at a Disney resort the sacrifices she made to get here. The self-imposed torture was undertaken because that spring Walt Disney, Visa, and Bank One joined forces to create a credit card that rewards subscribers with Disney Dream Dollars.

While such a cobranding alliance was new for Disney, it is hardly novel in the marketing world. A walk down supermarket aisles can attest to the fact that unions of at least two marketers to parent a product are common. There's Pantene hair dryers from Panasonic, General Mills' Sunkist fruit snacks, the Eddie Bauer version of the Ford Explorer, Hidden Valley Ranch flavor Wavy Lay's potato chips, and Betty Crocker Super Moist German Chocolate Cake Mix with Hershey's chocolate. Perhaps the most famous ingredient celebration—Intel and Pentium.

"The theory is that one plus one equals three," says Tom O'Donnell, senior vice president for relationship marketing at Bank One, which in the fall of 2003 also introduced a triple-branded card with Visa and Starbucks. "It means triple the awareness and triple the trust."

Women buy brands they know and trust. Brands move beyond their home base, extending to related markets to reap the benefits of that trust. Four of five successful new products are brand extensions, says Kirk Martensen, president of Chicago-based licensing consultancy Goldmarks.

There are now Coach watches and shoes, Cover Girl contact lenses and hair clips, Hummer shoes whose soles have the same tread design as its tire from EJ Footwear, and Mr. Clean cleaning gloves. PAC Paris is bringing out a line of Everlast fragrances, deodorants, and grooming aids. In 2003, Procter & Gamble licensed a Nature Made line of Olay vitamins to "close the link between inner beauty and outer beauty," says Olay Marketing Director Bill Brace.

At the same time, women are being seduced by store brands. Once stigmatized as lowbrow generics, these private-label goods are sizzling. One of every five items women purchase is now a store brand (in Europe it's two of every five items), and the wave is waxing. The more familiar women become with seeing store brands on the shelves, the likelier it is that they'll try them. ACNielsen estimated that in 2001 and 2002, unit sales of store-brand goods grew 8.6 percent, whereas national sales were up just 1.5 percent.

Costco's football stadium–sized warehouse stores carry the red, white, and black Kirkland Signature house brand—on everything from paper napkins to paprika to poultry. Wal-Mart's Ol' Roy dog food outsells Purina dog chow. (Together with its other store brands, which include such lines as Equate nasal spray and ibuprofen, Great Value beef jerky and bleach, Spring Valley vitamins, Sam's Choice tuna, and EverActive batteries, private-label merchandise accounts for around 40 percent of Wal-Mart's sales, according to *Private Label* magazine.) Half of all products at Target are private brands, including its Michael Graves line of housewares. 7-Eleven's house beer, Santiago, is taking on Corona.

Barnes & Noble stocks its own "house" books in better positions than books it carries from other publishers. Hundreds of items bear Rite Aid's new Pure Spring and 411 brands. Macy's, Inc., label is eclipsing Liz Claiborne. Albertsons supermarket is introducing its own premium brand called Essensia. Home Depot's Hampton Bay brand ceiling fans have sold so well that it added Hampton Bay lighting products. And gourmet grocer Trader Joe's Charles Shaw label wine (a.k.a. "Two-Buck Chuck") has gotten more media attention than many nationally advertised brands.

It is more than a price break in their favor. In many cases store brands are as good as, if not better than, nationally advertised brands. *Consumer Reports* ranked Winn-Dixie's chocolate ice cream ahead of Breyers and Kroger's potato chips superior to Ruffles and Pringles. Seventy percent of the people Gallup recently surveyed said that the quality of store brands was every bit as good as that of national brands. Now they are also so well designed with elegant labels and appealing packaging that the pricier "name" brand next to them can look positively frowzy in comparison.

No longer passive landlords of shelf space, retailers have become brand managers, full-fledged marketers, says Dan Stanek, executive vice president at consulting company Retail Forward. Because their own private-label products deliver better profits to them—and can differentiate them from rivals and engender shoppers' loyalty—retailers push them in shopper circulars and in-store displays. And this is important because, according to the Point-of-Purchase Advertising Bureau, almost three of every four (72 percent) purchasing decisions are made in the store.

20

The Devil You Know

Although they buy batteries on price, women *like* the Energizer Bunny. After a decade of hopping into TV commercials, the pink "spokes-hare" has become familiar. For this same reason, women warm to Absolut's more than two-decade-old bottle campaign, the milk-mustache ads launched in 1995, and "You're in good hands with Allstate."

Women may not always know what they like, but more often than not they like what they know: the recognizable, the vintage, the nostalgic. During tough times, many marketers try to move ahead by looking back.

"When we feel less secure, with less control over our daily lives, we reach out in brands to connect with a time when things seemed better, more comfortable," says Marc Gobé, president of Désgrippes Gobé Group, a New York–based corporate identity consulting company. "It's about finding security, what we can trust." Adds Marian Salzman, chief strategist at Euro RSCG, "Nostalgia for rosier days drives our appetite for retro products and design. Familiar is cozy, warm, and enveloping." It is also very effective.

Cashing in on nostalgia, Williams-Sonoma offers juice glasses with 1930s designs from French produce labels and Italian lamps from when electricity replaced gas. Pottery Barn features porcelain bathroom fixtures, wrought-iron beds, and a desk chair inspired by a 1929 schoolhouse chair. And in addition to Shaker and mission oak furniture, Hold Everything displays bathroom cabinets that look like they came from a 1931 dentist's office.

Volkswagen returned to its roots when it brought out the New Beetle several years ago. Breck shampoo, St. Joseph aspirin, and Sea & Ski sun-care lotion, which all but disappeared, have been revitalized. Levi's Type 1 jeans resemble those worn during the California gold rush. Coca-Cola brought back its trademark ribbon design, first developed 75 years ago.

On the ad front, PepsiCo brought back its jingles from the 1950s (voiced by Britney Spears). Sears reminded viewers that it sold their grandparents everything from farm equipment to saddle shoes—and has everything they want now from treadmills to "tankinis." "We didn't tell people to shop at Sears because it's been around for a long time," says Mark Figliulo, chief creative officer at Young & Rubicam, which fashioned the spots. "We reminded them that Sears is a trusted brand they can count on, that we had it then and we have it now." Ford, General Electric, and SC Johnson also pointed to their storied past—while assuring viewers they offer more than heritage.

The tub of talking Parkay first used in 1973 (to 1985) to suggest that the margarine tasted just like butter has been reborn with a contemporary wink—to poke fun at the idea that the tub can speak. Carly Simon's song "Anticipation" still speaks to those waiting for Heinz ketchup to drip on their burgers. Old Navy represents "The Brady Bunch" as "The Rugby Bunch" to sell sporty striped shirts.

"Spokescritters": Character Study

In a 1967 commercial, a lovable but underemployed Maytag repairman (Jesse White) taught trainees ways to pass the time with cards, crafts, and crossword puzzles. They had lots of time to pass—because the appliances they stood ready to service never broke down.

"Old Lonely," as the man in the blue uniform became known, is one of the longest-running brand icons in marketing. (Gordon Jump, who replaced Jesse White in 1988, retired in 2003 and was succeeded by Hardy Rawls.) Through various spots—in 1989, the only thing he gets to fix is lunch; in the 1980s, he gets a basset hound to stave off boredom; and in 2001, he gets an apprentice, who spends his time mulling Maytag's innovations—the icon has symbolized the single most relevant strategic idea in appliances—dependability.

For years, America's favorite fish, the tough-talking, scheming Charlie the Tuna (who may have had good taste but didn't taste good), surfaced from the briny deep, and ("Sorry") Charlie was cast back into it.

Since 1969, finicky feline Morris has purred petulantly for 9-Lives. The smart-alecky tabby plucked from an Illinois animal shelter was used to deflate cat owners' worry that their "children" won't eat.

The elves are still frolicking for Keebler's cookies—suggesting that the snacks come as close to homemade as you can get in a store. The Jolly Green Giant has been ho-ho-hoing for Pillsbury's vegetables since 1928, when he first appeared as a scowling hunchback in an untidy bearskin rug. The pale, pudgy Pillsbury Doughboy popped out in 1965, and Chester Cheetah took a catnap before returning as mascot for Frito-Lay's Cheetos. Mr. Clean, who reportedly was modeled on President Dwight D. Eisenhower, has been scouring for more than four decades. Tony has been roaring "Gr-r-r-eat" as the "spokestiger" for Kellogg's Frosted Flakes since 1951, and Snap, Crackle, and you-know-who have been popping for the cereal king since before the Great Depression.

The government legislated that the Marlboro Man ride off into the sunset, but many "spokescharacters" are still in the saddle, veritable golden geese. These fantasy folk heroes are by no means MTV hip, but women have embraced them like Linus blankets, "familiar, easy, comfortable, decisionless, which is particularly valuable for a shopper faced with a glut of similar products," says Cheryl Berman, president at the Leo Burnett agency, which has created more pop icons than any other agency. "Effective brand icons are characters with a story line, including friends, limitations, and fears."

Burnett's erstwhile creative director, Huntley Baldwin, says that the icons that demonstrate staying power all have a mission, a distinctive personality, a world all their own, and often a foil to draw viewers in. They are likeable—charming and disarming—but with a bit of an edge.

The agency's strategy has been not to look for a product's unique selling proposition—what about the widget that's special—but to find the generic appeal, the key benefit, the biggest idea in their categories, and make that brand-specific.

Research suggests that women cotton to these corny "spokescharacters" because they are nostalgic, fun to watch, and upbeat. The positive feelings that viewers have for the animated cartoons carry over into positive feelings for the product. Tests indicate that women recall commercials with "spokescritters" better than those with celebrities and are more easily persuaded to try a brand because of them. They were "invented as a way to make large, faceless manufacturers seem friendlier," says Will Ayres, managing director of creative at consultancy Enterprise IG in New York.

Through time, the mascots have been updated so as not to appear as if they are wallowing in an irrelevant past. The Pillsbury Doughboy was set gyrating to rap music in an attempt to keep him fresh. When Mr. Peanut was a dignified 87-year-old icon credited with elevating the crude peanut into an elegant party snack, Planters put him in surfer shorts and sandals, along with his requisite top hat and cane. (That bombed.) Soft and cuddly Snuggle, who first appeared in ads in 1983, lost his squeaky voice and high-pitched giggle to become a rogue anthropomorphic bear who wears sunglasses, dates models, and winks knowingly to the audience.

A few years ago, Charlie the Tuna became a fish du jour, strolling among tables of real people dining in a seaside restaurant, surfing the net, and drinking latte—but still not good enough for StarKist. And Geoffrey from Toys 'R Us was updated into a hip, wisecracking giraffe. Some said that he was too caustic for a toy-store brand.

"Change keeps consumers interested, but too much tampering and the character won't resonate with anyone," warns Burnett's Berman.

Interestingly, almost all these cute little animated TV stars, from Toucan Sam to Trix Rabbit to Budweiser's frogs to the California Raisins, are male. (Aunt Jemima, Betty Crocker, and Mrs. Butterworth are obvious exceptions.) A team from Southwest Texas State University wondered what would happen if the Energizer Bunny were female and determined that she most likely would be as effective and persuasive as male icons. In fact, they found that women were likelier to buy the product if the "spokescharacter" were a she.

21

Noah's Ark

The persistent white "spokesduck" first squawked "AFLAC" in January 2000 to remind viewers of the insurer's name. In one commercial, the quacker wandered into the bedroom of a couple considering starting a family and wound up under the sheets between them. In another spot, the orange-footed critter appeared outside the window of an airplane shouting "AFLAC!" (voice provided by comedian Gilbert Gottfried) to a forgetful passenger on the other side of the tiny portal.

The AFLAC duck seared its trademark catchphrase into women's minds just as the gecko did for Geico automobile insurance. The green computer-animated lizard that speaks with a British accent (Dave Kelly) has been trying to clear up the confusion over the similarity of their names since 1999. At the audition to be Geico's official mascot, one contender, the former Taco Bell Chihuahua mascot, is awestruck by the competition. "Oh great, a talking gecko," he moans.

While animals are virtual insurance to get women to pay attention—research demonstrates that women are much more receptive to these animal endorsers than men—insurance companies are not the only ones who have gone ape for them. All sorts of products beyond pet food have discovered that animals in ads are hard to forget and easy to love.

Advertising had been something of a Noah's ark long before the goofy-eyed Chihuahua blurted out, "Yo quiero Taco Bell." *He's* a direct descendant of Nipper, the little fox terrier designed to warm up RCA, the American Tourister ape who tossed luggage around to demonstrate that it is indestructible, and the reclusive koala bear who claimed that he hated Qantas for bringing so many people to see him.

Often marketers open the barn doors when they have nothing new to say about their products and just want to snag viewers' attention. (See, for example, Coca-Cola's animated polar bears in 1993 and Diet Coke's swimming elephants 2 years later.) Sometimes they function as metaphors to suggest a trait (the Energizer Bunny, persistence; the Lubriderm alligator, a warning about what your skin can turn into without it). Other times they can deliver a message that may sound ludicrous if said by a person. (The 7-Eleven sheep bleated "Latte" to set itself apart from trendsetters, and the Yellow Pages used an ostrich to represent people who never let their fingers do the walking.)

Using animals in ads isn't easy, as EDS discovered when it ran with the squirrels in Pamplona. (Trident also used squirrels, dispatching an angry one up the leg of a dentist who represents the one in five who *doesn't* recommend sugarless gum for patients who chew.)

To get those two daredevil baboons in the Sierra Mist ad to smile on camera, the trainer gently pushed their lips and rewarded them when they did it on their own. (To keep cool on a hot day at the zoo, one catapults the other into the nearby polar bear pool.) When an angry mountain biker raced down the cheetah that pilfered his Mountain Dew and reached down the cat's throat to retrieve it, the cat was baited to sprint by a tennis ball rigged on a motorized cable, and a robotic head was used when the biker appears to reach down the cheetah's throat.

The Merrill Lynch crew once resorted to howling, firing shotguns in the air, and hovering helicopters to get bulls to stampede. And that Pepsi-drinking chimp that broke out of a laboratory to party on the beach in 1994? The ape's trainer was hidden on the floor of the Jeep directing the ape when it drove. In 1998, it was a computer-generated goose that sky surfed, and Budweiser's talking frogs and Blockbuster's dancing rabbit (Carl) and guinea pig (Ray) also were computer-generated.

Ad makers grouse that when you use live animals (even trained ones), the ad winds up costing twice what you expect—and can take twice as long to film. However, advertising has gone to the dogs, cats, rhinos, geckos, and others because they are still relatively cheap to get and rarely have agents. And marketers don't have to fret about hair and makeup, multiculturalism, or political correctness or whether they smoked pot in college or will pose nude or land in some criminal pickle.

These animals hold the key to our cage because they make us laugh—without repercussions. They are fun to watch, and because they are innocent, we trust them. Psychologist Carol Moog has another theory. We all "want to feel loved unconditionally—even during a 30-second break," she says. "Nothing symbolizes unconditional love better than an animal."

22

A Word About Subliminal Advertising

Three decades ago, Wilson Bryan Key caused an uproar "exposing" subliminal advertising—the letters "*S E X*" in the ice cubes of a Gibley Gin ad and images of a penis in drawings of "spokescartoon" Joe Camel, for instance.

Today, covert messages designed to reach a particular audience within messages beamed at a larger group are an accepted element of advertising. Clever marketers use encryption to connect with certain people without risking alienating outsiders who don't get it. Call it subliminal advertising twenty-first-century style.

To telegraph that they are on the gay and lesbian wavelength, Borders Books and Coors Light beer featured pink triangles in their ads; Visa and Miller Lite used a rainbow-colored credit card and glass of beer, respectively. The symbols, meaningless to or unnoticed by the general population, resonate with gays. On billboards, Subaru bumpers bear the blue and yellow equals sign—the logo of gay advocacy group the Human Rights Campaign—and vanity license plates such as P-TOWNE (for the gay haunt Provincetown on Cape Cod in Massachusetts).

The inside joke is "like our little secret, clever, not offensive, and if you're in the know, you chuckle," explains Tim Bennett, marketing services manager at Subaru. And it avoids the backlash from conservatives that AT&T, American Airlines, and Anheuser-Busch have experienced wooing gays more overtly.

Other audiences are also reached via encrypted messages. "Whether to put a wedding ring on the model's finger is always a critical discussion in ad agencies; this subtle touch sends a targeting message," says Paul Kowal, president of Kowal Associates, a marketing consultancy in Boston. While ads featuring different nationalities are a beacon to those represented, marketers "often use lighter-skin blacks in mainstream venues to signal blacks without alienating whites," he says. In contrast, malt liquor advertising almost always uses blacks; "people see it as a black product." Car ads that subtly feature rifles and a shooting club in their backgrounds target National Rifle Association supporters, and the fish symbol on children's clothing targets Christians.

Focus on subliminal advertising first erupted in 1957 when market researcher James Vicary reported that he had invented a technique to get people to buy stuff they didn't consciously desire. Vicary claimed to have induced audiences in a New Jersey drive-in theater to buy 58 percent more popcorn and 18 percent more Coke by flashing the very brief, consciously undetectable phrases, "Hungry? Eat popcorn" and "Drink Coca-Cola," periodically over the movie *Picnic.*

These results could not be verified or reproduced, but they were quickly decried as brainwashing. Then, in 1972, Wilson Bryan Key's *Subliminal Seduction* and *Media Sexploitation* contended that advertisers regularly sneak hard-to-detect sexual imagery in ads. Soon after, when controversy erupted over a TV ad for memory game Husker Du that flashed the words, "Get it," for a nanosecond, the Federal Communications Commission (FCC) banned subliminal messages on air.

More recently, supermarkets have admitted that they have embedded "Do not steal" messages in in-store music and dual-track audiotapes and have planted subliminal messages under soothing seagull sounds designed to motivate women to "Think thin" or get hopping, "The early bird gets the worm." University of Washington researcher Anthony Greenwold found that such messages increased self-esteem or memory but only as a result of the "power of suggestion" made to the conscious mind, not to the unconscious.

23

In the Store

Modern marketers, in an attempt to psych out women shoppers, have prodded, poked, and surveyed them; scanned their checkout tapes; coded their coupons; traced their steps; and filmed their in-store antics. Thus they have found that almost 70 percent of women's purchases are impulsive and often triggered by where things are in the store.

Usually, the more shopper-employee contact there is, the more time a woman spends in the store, and the more deeply she gets pulled into it, the greater is the average sale, says retail anthropologist Paco Underhill, chairman of New York–based Envirosell, Inc., a market research firm, and author of the best-seller *Why We Buy.* Women spend an average of 12 minutes and 57 seconds in a supermarket; men spend 9 minutes and 39 seconds. To keep men longer, Underhill advises treating them "like small children," say, by playing loud music.

To discourage "drive-by shopping" most supermarkets put essentials such as milk in the rear and dairy products and produce on different sides of the store so that women must pass nonessentials to get to them. These stores typically sell 30 percent more than those configured otherwise.

Underhill's tapes show that most women turn right when they enter a store, so retailers usually showcase promotions there. Customers tend to avoid product displays just inside the door, an area Underhill calls the "decompression zone." Evidence shows that merchandise at eye level generally sells much better than goods higher or lower on the shelves; that even if they won't drink it for a week, shoppers prefer to buy cold soda than soda at room temperature; and that angled shelves are far more effective than flat ones.

It's no wonder that magazines at checkout and sweaters on counters so often look dog-eared and shopworn. They are handled (or manhandled) on average of nine times before they are bought. American women may be the most tactile in the world, says Underhill. This is why retailers such as Banana Republic and The Gap display their wares on tables—so women can "pet" them.

Touch can be a turn-off, too. Underhill's "butt brush" theory holds that women in narrow aisles are less comfortable than those in wider aisles, where there's less chance of being touched or feeling crowded. Fear of being brushed keeps them from examining merchandise displayed below waist level. On the other hand, standing at the corner of a department store cosmetics counter where they can wrap themselves around the angle and nestle in a bit is conducive to sales. Along the main stretch of the counter a few feet away is not. Receipts are also higher at stores with recessed cul-de-sacs, nooks, and crannies that let shoppers stand clear of passing traffic and browse without interruption; at secure interior "dwell" zones in airport gift shops, away from the "grab and go" zone near the cash register; and at rear seating in fast-food outlets. Women gravitate there, whereas men choose tables up front. (When alone, however, women usually use the drive-thru.)

Women, it seems, study the packages of new products before they buy. (According to one study, 91 percent of all drugstore buyers read the front of a package, 42 percent read the back, and 8 percent read the sides. Sixty-three percent of women who bought something read at least one product package.) Reading takes time—and aisle space. Women generally take longer to decide to buy than men do, says

Allen Konopacki, president of Incomm Center for Research and Sales Training in Chicago.

Women also are influenced by the track piped in, even if they do not exactly listen to it. Not long ago what was playing was for the entertainment of employees. Now it is audio merchandising, and Old Navy, Starbucks, and others sell the tapes they play. What's playing changes based on the predictability of who shops when. At 10:30 on Saturday mornings, baby boomers dominate, so their music plays then, Underhill says. At 7:30 P.M., gen-Xers flood in, so it's time for younger sounds.

Light is also a marketing mechanism. Two-thirds of shoppers visit malls after 5:30 P.M. but leave when they see the sun setting, says Robert Gibbs, founder of Gibbs Planning, a mall design company based in Birmingham, Michigan. His firm adds lighting around sky-lights and windows to hide the sunset.

Although in the store women have become more like men—hurried, hit-and-runners shoppers instead of dedicated browsers and searchers—they still relish the social aspects of shopping. Two women in a store can be a shopping machine. Studies show that they often spend more time and money than one woman shopping alone—and certainly more than when a guy tags along. "Bring-a-friend, get-a-discount" promotions and seating areas just outside dressing rooms encourage this social aspect.

Retailers aren't ignoring the get-it-done-fast reality, however. Sixty percent of shoppers today call themselves time-pressed and purpose-driven compared with 43 percent in 2000, according to the International Council of Shopping Centers. Waiting time in stores is the single most important factor in customer satisfaction.

To this end, more retailers have instituted self-checkout, and more cash registers can complete the credit-card transaction with-out carbon copies, says Gibbs. In spring 2003, MasterCard began test-ing a "contactless" PayPass that even eliminates the need to swipe the card. More stores are cramming as many products as possible under one roof to provide one-stop shopping convenience—and keep the customer within their walls longer.

They are also abbreviating signs (which get, on average, less than 2 seconds of exposure per customer) and posting them where shoppers are most likely to see them. "Putting a sign that requires 12 seconds to read in a place where customers spend 4 seconds isn't much more effective than putting it in your garage," sniffs Underhill. He claims that what people most look at is other people. Therefore, the best signs in fast-food restaurants are above the registers, at the level of the cashier's face.

Cultural anthropologists have found the differences in how the sexes shop. At the grocery store—more a sensual orgy now than a superchore—women scrutinize the radicchio to make sure that there's no blemish. In electronics shops they quiz the clerk and leave the brochure unruffled. Oddly, when it comes to hardware and software, the sexes swap roles: Men browse and wander, whereas women are purposeful and directed.

At the mall, women often compare items and envision their prospective purchase in use. At Nordstrom's, the departments are labeled "Savvy" and "Individualist." Men's departments are simply called "Men's Suits" and "Men's Furnishings." Most of what women take into the dressing room stays there. If a store can get a guy to try it on, it's just about sold.

A dressing room "is the closing place where the sale happens," says Underhill. Stores can increase this likelihood by installing flattering lighting, making the rooms sufficiently ample to turn around in and park a stroller, and adding a place for a companion to sit and something for him or her to do (toys for kids or magazines for men). The room also must be warm, comfortable, and clean.

Most retailers think that their success is tied to their merchandise, says Mary Lou Quinlan, chief executive officer of Just Ask a Woman strategic consultancy. "But customers think [that] it's about service and the personality and brand persona of the store." Sales staff must be polite, friendly, and knowledgeable. The store itself must be pristine, simple, and organized. "Women notice *everything*," she adds.

24

A Dozen Tricks
Marketers Play

On a recent visit to Atlanta, the bathroom scale in room 1115 of the Ritz Carlton registered 4 pounds less than my true and verifiable weight. Had I shed some excess baggage, I wondered? Had house-keeping accidentally underset the scale? Or was this a deliberate and clever mind game the hotel was playing? Its motive seemed clear: A pampered guest would feel better about her costly stay—and perhaps be more inclined to indulge from their menu. Ah, temptation!

It's no secret that advertisers use various techniques from focus groups to "thematic apperception tests" to card sorts to sentence-completion drills to brand "obituaries" and cultural-anthropological analyses to hide persuasions to buy. They are all around us. Shops spritz floral fragrance and supermarkets magnify the whiff of fresh baked bread because evidence suggests that customers browse longer and buy more in shops filled with such olfactory temptations. Some stores use lavender essence to relax shoppers; others use stimulating bergamot oil to get them excited. Casinos pump in oxygen to keep gamblers awake and scents of peppermint and vanilla to keep them enthralled, and slot machine play is up.

Years ago, Vance Packard, author of *Hidden Persuaders*, saw demonic intent in these marketers' use of environmental cues. Today, we accept these subtle inducements as an inevitable part of modern life, as prevalent but unnoticed as acid rain.

Even overtly visual triggers aren't often recognized. Years ago, the late color researcher Carlton Wagner conducted blind tests, putting the same coffee in four different colored canisters. Women who sampled the coffee found that the brew from the yellow canister tasted weak; from the chocolate canister, too strong; from the blue canister, too mild; but from the red can, bingo, it was "rich."

Pastries from a pink box taste better than from any other colored box, he discovered, and people willingly pay more for them—as well as cosmetics packaged in pink. Blue connotes authority and respect and explains why police and trial lawyers' "uniforms" are navy. Purple conveys luxury and indulgence, whereas green and yellow packaging implies freshness.

Color can tempt and discriminate simultaneously. Bright orange signals democratic affordability—as Howard Johnson well knew. However, poor people walk right by forest green and burgundy store awnings: to them, those colors signal pricey exclusivity.

The price tag itself often sends more than a rational message. Most prices end with a nine to make shoppers feel that they are getting a bargain. On the other hand, experts say that people regard products with whole dollar prices such as $10 or $100 as higher quality and classier than if they were offered at $9.99 or $99.99. Because we process numbers from left to right, even trained bargain hunters perceive $1.99 as significantly cheaper than $2.

Chances are that a retailer's or restaurant's soundtrack has more sad, slow songs than upbeat fast ones because research shows that people eat more when fast music plays, but they drink and buy more when listening to lower-key ballads, especially those in a major key instead of atonal or dissonant tunes. The ideal tempo to induce sales: 70 to 110 beats per minute.

Fashion retailers tend to play music associated with a Saturday night out to put shoppers in a good mood and to make being in their stores more fun. (One study found that if classical music was played in a wine store rather than Muzak, customers bought pricier wines.) TV banks showing exciting music videos make shoppers feel hyped up.

The seduction continues in the try-on room with softer, flattering lighting to make skin look healthy and "trick" mirrors that make the customer look taller and slimmer.

Few retailers have clocks on the wall by design. If you are aware of the time, you will be reminded just how long you've been shopping—and spending.

It's a misconception that nobody wants to wait in line. Envirosell President Paco Underhill says that checkout lines should be long enough to create "laudable crowding" but not so long that people consider abandoning what they had planned to buy. According to Underhill, a shoe salesman who gets his customer seated has a 20 to 50 percent greater likelihood of making the sale.

Coupons may be as much about temptation as cents off. People resent the clipping and organizing (hence the clipless coupon), but each year more than three out of four of us cash them in. It's not just because rationally they reduce the risk of trying something new and make us feel as if we are beating the system. It's that they create an emotional high: Using coupons makes women feel like good homemakers, diligently taking care of their families.

25

Don't Even Think About It: A Dozen Ploys Bound to Backfire

Marketers are targeting women, but not all their messages arrive as intended. Here are some tactics that are bound to miscarry.

One

Sexy ads are fine. Ads that feature women as sex objects are not. Buxom babes and frat-boy raucousness *can* sell beer. But Miller Lite's salacious "catfights" between two sexy bimbos who tear each other's clothes off while wrestling in a trough of cement crossed the line. In versions of the "taste great, less filling" argument aired on cable, *Playboy* playmate Kitana Baker tells model/actresses Tanya Ballinger, "Let's make out." Then viewers learn that it's all a fantasy of two guys at a bar.

Women weren't amused by the sex-inspired parody of beer and babe commercials; neither were most men to whom they pandered. Ironically, for years, former parent Philip Morris had barred Miller from running ads with women rolling in Jell-O because the company considered it disrespectful.

The National Organization for Women (NOW) agreed. Lisa Bennett, communications director of NOW, said that women disdain the vulgarity of Miller's beer and babes clawing commercials. They also bristle at more subtle sexual innuendoes that thinly disguise misogyny. Anheuser-Busch's three-armed man grabbing a woman's behind and a guy's dream of dating both his girlfriend and her roommate are cases in point, Bennett says.

Two

Calvin Klein's fragrance Obsession portrayed a negative concept in a powerful and positive way. Ads that focus on women's unnatural obsessions, such as an overweaning preoccupation with the cleanliness of their toilet bowls, can't transcend that negativity. Real women do not relate to the sniveling, helpless, insecure, and indecisive creatures some advertisers serve up any more than they can relate to superconfident superwomen who need only rely on themselves.

In their own ways, they are both as unnatural and unapproachable as the egg-shell-skinned women in the L'Oreal Mineral ad with flashing metallic gold and purple eyes, a dripping red vampirish mouth, stiffly gelled hair, and silvery purple nails.

Showing beautiful, ultrathin women is also risky. Laurie Mintz, associate professor of educational and counseling psychology at the University of Missouri–Columbia, found that women were more depressed and dissatisfied with their bodies after seeing ads with such creatures. Today, the ideal ad model is an accomplished pragmatist. And Jenny Craig learned soon after it hired—and then fired—Monica Lewinsky that fame is not a sufficient connector. The White House intern generated attention, but her endorsement didn't encourage women to sign on. They did not see her as genuine, admirable, or trustworthy.

Ally McBeal was an engaging TV protagonist, but as an advertising "shero," she would have been a zero. Her obsession with marriage, hopeless neurosis, and discontentedness and powerlessness to choose the lifestyle she wanted canceled out her sexiness, intelligence, and success.

Three

Sure, women want to be able to relate to the characters in ads, but they also want to understand what the product offers. Sometimes this gets lost when an advertiser uses "$10 words" when "5-cent"ones will do. When people are robbed, they call a cop, not a law enforcement officer, says marketing consultant Al Ries. And no one says, "Let's go to a financial services company to get our finances serviced" when they mean a bank.

Aiming to be politically correct, marketers often inflate their language to the point that a message becomes unwieldy, confusing, or alienating. UPS changing from parcel delivery to "Synchronizing the World of Commerce" may get people to think that it is going into the watch business, Ries cautions. Boston Chicken stumbled here when it added turkey, meatloaf, ham, and other items to the menu and became Boston Market. "Everyone knows what a chicken dinner is, but who knows what a market dinner is?" he wonders.

Four

Marketers who pitch superfluous benefits rather than real ones, such as the 1960s car ads that emphasized color or whitewall tires or contemporary spots that claim that the sun never sets on a banking empire (why would you care if you're in Dubuque?), risk passing their pursued like ships in the night.

In a chat room recently, Intuition razor's commercial was denounced for exaggerating a problem to comical proportions. In the ad, several women suffer discomfit and indignity shaving: Soap flies out of one's hand, razors nick another's ankles, and a third loses her balance in the bathroom, while, Jewel, "that sellout," bops out Intuition in the background. The gizmo, which combines razor, shaving cream, and blades all in one neat place, provides a real benefit, but the problem it pretends to solve is ludicrous. "Leg shaving is *not that* difficult or something to get *that* excited about," one woman huffed. "Lather 'em up, scrape 'em off, moisturize if you like, and get on with your day. I've never had soap go flying out of *my* hands while shaving my legs."

Women don't want lifestyle; they want life—life that is rich, rewarding, and exciting. They can sniff out when they are being played for a sucker, as drug companies increasingly do by inventing problems. "Social anxiety disorder," for example, a.k.a. shyness, "a benign personality trait once viewed as becoming in some people, is today being cast as a prevalent medical problem, relieved by a powerful psychotropic drug like Paxil," said Dr. Scott Gottlieb, a New York internist. Too many pills are prescribed for too many soft diagnoses because of marketing, he says, noting that "minimal brain damage" became "attention deficit disorder" and "hyperactivity disorder" for marketing purposes. "Economics have replaced curiosity as the driving force behind research," complained Gottlieb. "Cashing in on the real and imaginary health anxieties of Americans is a lucrative business."

Ads that tout a company's tradition and hierarchy, without providing a reason customers should consider the company, fall into the same trap. While women like the reliability of well-established companies, they know that such companies represent an old order that historically has excluded them, and they are suspicious of big. Then, too, while they respect core brands and values, they want to discover them on their own instead of wearing their mom's Chanel No. 5 or driving their father's Oldsmobile or taking the word of some white-coated authority figure. If the marketing involves a sellout, they are even more indignant. The American Medical Association got a real shiner a few years ago when it sold its seal of approval to Sunbeam health care products for hefty royalties. Women today subscribe to the guide at their side instead of the sage on the stage.

Five

Ads that try too hard often come off like the adolescent boy wearing his hat backward. Over-the-top antics or high-tech production values catch women's eyes but not necessarily their wallets. When "the nation's innkeeper" tried to tell the world about its $1 billion renovation to better compete with the Hiltons, Marriotts, and Sheratons of the world, Holiday Inn showed a voluptuous woman turning heads as she strode through a 20-year class reunion. A voiceover intoned the cost of such body enhancements as a nose job and breast implants. An old classmate who claims he never forgets a face struggles to recall hers—and cringes as he realizes he's looking at Bob Johnson. "It's amazing, the changes you can make for a few thousand dollars," a voiceover explains. "Imagine what Holiday Inn will look like when we spend a billion." A traditional, homespun, vanilla ice cream, apple pie, middle-American brand had stepped way out of character with gender-bending content that tried so hard to be witty that it boomeranged.

Six

Humor works if it is used to explain a specific product benefit, not to be gratuitously mean or mock a cherished value or institution. In the emotional days following 9/11, Kenneth Cole's "God Dress America!" billboard hitched its wagon to the terrorist attacks in a tasteless way that seemed to mock the moment and the prevailing sentiments of patriotism, solidarity, and seriousness.

An ad where a widow is devastated not by her husband's death but by the fact that he is being buried in their beloved car is done in by its dark humor, says Jody Moxham, president of ad research company PhaseOne.

Seven

Marketing that makes fun of personal traits that make consumers self-conscious, such as a raspy Fran Drescher voice or an overly ample Queen Latifah dress size, or that portrays people as down on their luck or sadistic alienates its audience. Toyota's "Key Party" doesn't open the right doors. The male swingers look scared when a fat woman routs through a bowl. She'll go "upstairs" with the owner of the car keys she's fished out. However, when she extracts the keys to a Corolla, the guys leap up, their zeal to be associated with this car surpassing disgust for the woman.

Gross behavior—Jenny on the john—or rude noises such as belching or farting only work when the target is teens, says PhaseOne's Moxham. Hip British clothing company French Connection's edgy ads based on its initials and home country (FCUK) and the Broadway play *Urinetown* generated attention, but both had steep negatives to overcome.

In the 2000 winter Olympics, runner Suzy Hamilton escapes a chainsaw murderer as "Why sport?" flashed on the screen, followed by "You'll live longer." Nike intended to spoof a horror movie, but women took it as mocking violence against them. Nike landed in another pickle soon after when it promised that its ACG Air Goat shoe would help the runner avoid trees and becoming a "drooling, misshapen nonextreme trail-running husk of my former self. Forced to roam the earth in a motorized wheelchair with my name, embossed on one of those cute little license plates you get at carnivals or state fairs, fastened to the back." Women found it cruel and crass, not cute and convincing.

And Budweiser bombed with women in a spot where a young man's friend tells him to check out his girlfriend's mom to see how the girlfriend will look 20 years from now. Mom looks great through the peephole, but when she enters, her gigantic butt fills the screen.

Eight

Messages that stereotype by ethnicity or sex often bomb. Retailer Just for Feet's dimwitted and baffling commercial demonstrated foot-in-mouth disease and came off as racist and wildly insensitive. Four white men in a Humvee track a barefoot Kenyan runner, as if in an animal safari, knock him out with dope-laced water, and force sneakers onto his feet. When the bewildered tribesman awakens, he's horrified and desperately tries to tear off the unwanted footwear. *Advertising Age* vilified it as "neocolonialist . . . culturally imperialist, and certainly condescending" and questioned the sanity of its creators. The *Des Moines Register* said that it made Denny's and Texaco (who'd earlier been censured for coarse discrimination against African-Americans) "look like abolitionists."

Of late, more and more the stereotype is of an incompetent, helpless, clueless guy, the buffoon who scorches the breakfast sausages and ruins the laundry by mixing whites and darks and who is saved by the calm, competent (and possibly contemptuous) wife. This is marketers pandering to women whom they believe nurture a historical grudge and welcome themselves in the dominant mother-child role. In a Visa spot, a couch potato slob points out a spot his wife missed cleaning. She turns the vacuum cleaner hose on him.

Most ads that offend were never intended to do so. Canon doctored a spot in which a smart-aleck seventh grader snipped that her mom's presentation was "stone-aged" after women complained about the child's rudeness. Canon had meant the exchange as friendly mother-daughter banter.

Before political correctness hijacked marketing, it would have taken a full-scale boycott to can a costly campaign. Now companies retreat at a whiff of trouble. Pennsylvania mom Sharon Smith, whose 18-year-old daughter had died of a heroin overdose, was horrified to see a Christian Dior's Addict perfume ad in which a trim woman looked like she needed a fix. Smith objected, and Dior changed the scent's name and advertising.

Nine

Women like to play, but they don't like to be toyed with. When the Department of Homeland Security warned Americans to tape their windows and stock up on bottled water, women were scared silly. When they figured out that they were pawns in a political game, they got miffed. Fear is a great motivator, but if the marketer's slip is showing, women see it.

They swallow lots of serotonin uptake inhibitors but distrust the drug companies that make them. This mistrust intensified after revelations that women were, in effect, dutiful guinea pigs in hormone-replacement therapy (HRT) experiments. Now findings that suggest that HRT causes more problems than it corrects or prevents are being questioned, and women are left wondering what to do.

Anytime women sense that they are being manipulated, their backs go up. When John Nuveen & Company showed the paralyzed Christopher Reeve rising from his wheelchair and walking (by virtue of attaching his face to an ambulatory body) to celebrate amazing things in the future, women were intrigued. When the Chicago-based investment firm with no connection to medical research then asked, "What amazing things can you make happen?" and encouraged viewers to "leave your mark," they became appalled at being exploited. Like a Jerry Lewis telethon, the spot was designed to elicit tears. Unlike the cerebral palsy fund-raiser, this wasn't for a socially beneficial cause but for corporate coffers.

Benetton has abandoned "shockvertising," or at least toned it down, because audiences resented the company's maudlin maneuvers. Instead of death row inmates, dying AIDS sufferers, and a nun and priest kissing, it has taken to showing respectful images of the world's poor. Its "Food for Life" ads "put a face on hunger and demonstrate that Benetton has grown up," says Lucy Farey-Jones, head of strategic planning at San Francisco's Venables, Bell & Partners ad agency.

Even companies that concentrate on concepts women consider important, such as safety, often hit the wrong tone. Just Ask a Woman Chief Executive Officer May Lou Quinlan says that ads showing crash-test dummies undamaged after being slung through a steering wheel as their auto slams into a concrete wall are less soothing to a mom than Detroit intended.

Ten

Ads that pay homage to another time date themselves. Take the movie *Bachelor* from a few years back. Showing the eligible man chased by dozens of desperate would-be wives played to an old stereotype. So did a Bankrate.com ad suggesting that women need to trick men into marriage. A smiling, pregnant bride about to cut the wedding cake stands beside her morose groom. "Less than 2 percent of condoms actually fail," reads the headline. "Every percent counts . . . no commitment required," concludes the text.

Another surefire way to derail is by using words that have become clichés through overuse. *Cool,* for example, has become a lot less cool, just like the once-popular smiley face, because of its ubiquity.

Eleven

Marketers may penetrate women's radar screens with omission but never by commission. Lying is the ultimate insult, punishable by withdrawal of trust, as Sony Pictures learned in June 2001. While movie marketers selectively pick raves and bury pans when they reprint critics' blurbs, Sony's flimflam went further: It provided phony reviews by a phony critic.

The fictitious David Manning of the real *Ridgefield Press,* a small weekly in Connecticut, praised Sony's *A Knight's Tale, The Animal, Vertical Limit,* and *Hollow Man* when it was actually Sony's marketing department that penned the accolades—and invented Manning. Connecticut's Consumer Protection Commissioner summed it up this way: "What Sony did was like having a chef pose as a food critic and then give his own restaurant four stars."

Women *want* to believe the ads they see. When they discover that they can't, they dismiss *all* the claims the tricky advertiser makes. Clorox Company did itself more harm than good with ads in which animated goldfish talk in upside-down side-by-side Glad-Lock and Ziploc bags. The fish in SC Johnson's Ziploc bag is in trouble: His bag is leaking, and he asks for help—to borrow a cup of water. But Clorox was found guilty of misrepresenting its rival and publicly humiliated.

On the Web recently a cybercitizen bemoaned a chart she'd seen at a Hyundai dealer. It inaccurately compared Hyundai's Santa Fe model with Honda's CRV and Toyota's RAV4. "Why would a company bring itself up by lying about its competition?" she grumbled. "They must be embarrassed about what they have to offer."

Twelve

"Ring around the collar" worked for years with its insight that women check the necklines on their guys' shirts. However, its tattle-tale whine soon diffused the magic of sharing that dirty little secret. It became annoying, in the same way that Mr. Whipple's penchant for Charmin squeezing did.

For fear of annoying, companies have scaled back on e-mail blasts, telemarketing (even before the do not call registry went into effect), and online pop-ups (despite the automatic setting on Windows XP). IVillage discovered that 92.5 percent of its community found pop-ups the most frustrating feature of the Web.

Smart marketers also have stopped yelling. Remember ranting, red-faced Crazy Eddie or bombastic Jacko for Energizer? Women would much rather listen to a soft-spoken announcer who calmly tells of a sale going on that might interest them than an in-your-face salesman (or Web site) screaming the price and promising the best deal in town.

And while we're at it, they also resent salesmen butting in when they are speaking, dismissing their concerns and turning their points of discussion into challenges to conquer. Rather, to win them, experts recommend making eye contact (which men often avoid for fear it signals intimacy or confrontation) and nodding, smiling, and offering an occasional "mmm" or "uh-huh," body language to signal that they have been heard.

Gazing into
the Crystal Ball

Recently, in describing its positioning, Sears Roebuck claimed that it does *not* anticipate what its customers want; it "reflects the world of middle America and all of its desires and concerns and problems and faults."

This is pious-sounding but puerile thinking. "By not anticipating, Sears allowed retailers such as Wal-Mart, Home Depot, and Target to carve out gigantic chunks of its bread-and-butter business," snipped *Ad Age* President Rance Crain. He went on to question whether a retailer, "or any business for that matter, can get very far by not trying to figure out what its customers are going to want."

Whether they turn out to be stargazing or naval gazing, here are 15 predictions for anticipatory marketers.

1. Little Men

As women solidify their dominance, shattering the now-cracked glass ceiling, men will be reduced to househusbands, pets, and sex toys, a shadow of their former selves. They will take over the "pink ghettoes," continuing the conversion of stewardesses to flight attendants and secretaries to executive assistants. With two in five women believing that they are superior to men and many choosing not to have a family, independent think tank Demos predicts a "crisis in masculinity," with reverse discrimination likely. Some people even predict that technology will reengineer men to bear babies!

2. For Love, Not Money

Forget prenuptial agreements; marriages routinely will come with time-limit contracts. As women become increasingly financially self-sufficient, they won't need marriages of economics. Men will have to earn their keep in nonfiscal ways. *Old maids* won't be a derogatory term. "People will stay unmarried and childless until their late thirties or forties, or even permanently—by choice," says Ira Matathia, managing director of Euro RSCG.

3. Focus, Not Balance

Balance may be what's on women's agenda today; tomorrow it may be focus. Indeed, Ford Motor Company's small Focus was designed to connect with young people by representing a value critical to them—"living in the moment and mindfulness," says Jan Klug, marketing communications manager of Ford Division.

4. Time Off for Good Behavior

Menopausal may be replaced by "work-pausal" as women take sabbaticals midcareer. Time out won't just mean taking a breather; it will mean discovering new skills to master different careers. Shorter respites may *feel* longer as science creates pharmaceutical and bioneural ways to alter our perception of time and make an hour off feel like a week.

5. Three Lives in One

A generation ago, when middle age began at 35, a Clairol commercial urged women to go blond because with only one life to lead, didn't they want to have more fun? Blondes may indeed have more fun, but the premise crumbles when it is realized that women, like cats, have *many* lives to lead. With 20 years added to midlife, they will constantly reinvent themselves. One of those lives likely will be as an entrepreneur small-business owner. Others will involve active volunteerism and mentorship.

6. An Uncertain Age

In the next half century, the number of American women aged 55 years and older will double. It might not be so easy to tell because they will glow with youth and vitality. While most people already think of themselves as 10 to 15 years younger than they really are chronologically, with surgical nip and tucks everyone could look at least 10 years younger. People won't say she looks good for her age; they'll say she looks good (period).

As the white majority narrows, feminine beauty will be redefined from tall and thin and usually blond to include different races, ages, and body shapes.

7. Femme Families

Even with an accent on individualism, there will be a new awakening to community, especially womencentric ones. More lonely widows and divorcees will band together, sharing hobbies, travel, and entertainment. Dressing for success will mean dressing that pleases other women. The definition of family will broaden to include blended households, gay parents, and extended communities of friends and housemates. New housing structures will combine communal features with private quarters.

8. The Last Taboo Takes It on the Chin

Talk of aging and dying has long been anathema in youth-obsessed America, but this taboo is dying. "Conscious aging says the big adventure is the inner journey, and that does not have to stop when you can no longer ski downhill," said Rick Moody, ex-director of the Brookdale Center on Aging at Hunter College in New York and author of *The Five Stages of the Soul.* At the same time, marketers increasingly will tune their radar to religion, and the Supreme Being will become the top endorser.

9. Ad-Free Zones

As advertising becomes ubiquitous, consumers will pay to elude it. TiVo has its foot in the door of commercial-free zones. Marketers also will trade services or vouchers for people's willingness to hear their ads or participate in their marketing exercises. Phone companies already award talk time to users who listen to (and respond to questions about) called-in ads, and marketers subsidize parking for car owners who drive ad-emblazoned vehicles.

10. More Technical Customization

Faith Popcorn envisions a future in which toothpaste is prepared based on the reading of a sensor in a woman's pillow of the acid and alkaline factors in her mouth. Similarly, our meals could be assembled robotically based on what nutrients the detectors reveal we are missing, and the fridge naturally will be filled telepathically.

11. Show Me the Money

Pricing in the future won't be based on what the market will bear but on what each of us will individually offer to pay for something. Barter will be back big time. Retailers will experiment with variable pricing, providing lower prices during slow shopping periods and charging a premium for personal shoppers, home delivery, and other individualized services.

12. Magic (and Impatience) Will Become Commonplace

The tempo of expectation will quicken. This means speedier connections and instant feedback. (Internet connections that take longer than a second will be too annoying.) And in an ever faster-moving society, we'll increasingly embrace a "magic bullet" approach to health and appearance. Lunch-hour face lifts will be a norm for women attuned to fast-drying nail polish, hair coloring on the go, and instant fat removal.

13. Barbie's Back

As women grow increasingly comfortable with themselves, nonpressured femininity will make a comeback. And women who hid their femininity behind business suits will let it show. This means that it will be okay, even fun, to do "girly" things—without guilt. Indulgences now secretly savored will be out of the closet—along with dolls and doilies.

14. Pushing the Fertility Envelope

In the Bible, the long-barren Sarah became a mother in her nineties. Science will continue to come up with ways to extend the biological clock. Other advances in women's health will multiply as cures are found for breast and ovarian cancer. Women increasingly will act as their own physicians, taking home diagnostic tests and prescribing alternative medicines to heal themselves. And women who watched amazed as Viagra was covered initially by insurance while birth control pills weren't will no longer settle for that.

15. An Educated Consumer Is the Best Customer

Discount retailer Syms clothing store coined it first, but increasingly, the consumer mantra of tomorrow will be "Know everything about everything." EURO RSCG's Strategy Director Marian Salzman says that "before digging into a container of coleslaw, consumers will demand to know where the cabbage was grown, how the soil was fertilized, how the mayonnaise was manufactured, and even where the eggs that went into it were hatched."

Index

About the Author

Bernice Kanner is a marketing expert with Bloomberg L.P., a columnist for *Marketwatch*, and the editor-in-chief of *Women'sBizUS*. In addition, she is the author of *Are You Normal About Sex, Love, and Relationships* (2004); *The Super Bowl of Advertising: How the Commercials Won the Game* (2003); *Are You Normal About Money?* (2001); *The 100 Best TV Commercials and Why They Worked* (1999); *Lies My Parents Told Me* (1996); and *Are You Normal?* (1995), which was featured on *Oprah*. Kanner has appeared widely as a marketing expert, and from 1981 through 1994 she wrote the award-winning "On Madison Avenue" column appearing in *New York* magazine. She and her husband, son, and daughter live in New York City and Bridgewater, Connecticut.